WOMAN'S WEEKLY

CLASSIC
KNITS

WOMAN'S WEEKLY

CLASSIC KNITS

HAMLYN

First published in Great Britain in 1994 by Hamlyn
an imprint of Reed Consumer Books Limited
Michelin House, 81 Fulham Road
London SW3 6RB
and Auckland, Melbourne, Singapore and Toronto

Art Director **Jacqui Small**
Senior Executive Editor **Judith More**
Executive Art Editor **Larraine Shamwana**
Editor **Jennifer Jones**
Design **Town Group Consultancy Ltd**
Production **Michelle Thomas**
These patterns have all appeared in *Woman's Weekly*.

A CIP record for ths book is available from the British Library.

ISBN 0 600 58563 8

Produced by Mandarin Offset
Printed and bound in Hong Kong

WOMEN

MEN

CHILDREN

COUNTRY CLASSIC

A SLIMLINE, COUNTRY-STYLE SWEATER FOR HER

MEASUREMENTS To fit sizes 86-91 (97-102) cm/34-36 (38-40) in.

Actual measurement 104 (120) cm/41 (47¼) in. **Side seam** Both sizes 42.5 cm/16¾ in.

Length 69 (69.5) cm/27 (27¼) in. **Sleeve seam** Both sizes 44 cm/17¼ in.

MATERIALS
6 (7) 100 g balls of House of Fraser Classic D.K.; No. 8 (4 mm) and No. 10 (3¼ mm) knitting needles; a cable needle. Yarn: used Cream.

TENSION
25 stitches and 31 rows, to 10 x 10 cm/4 x 4 in, over the pattern, using No. 8 (4 mm) needles.

NOTE
Instructions are given for 86-91 cm/34-36 in size. Where they vary, work figures in round brackets for larger size. Work instructions in square brackets as stated after the 2nd bracket.

WOMEN

This traditional sweater has dropped shoulders and a round neck. It is knitted in bobble, twist and cable panels, with twist rib borders. The yarn is machine-washable, acrylic/wool/nylon D.K.

BACK

With No. 10 (3¼mm) needles cast on 110 (122) sts and work in twisted rib as follows:
1st rib row: P2, [cr2rt, p2] to end. **2nd rib row:** K2, [p2, k2] to end. Repeat the last 2 rows, 3 times more, then the 1st row again. **Inc row:** Rib 7 (6), inc, [rib 4 (3), inc] to last 7 sts, rib to end – 130 (150) sts. ******
Change to No. 8 (4 mm) needles and work the 8-row pattern as follows:
1st row: P2, cr2rt, p2, k3, p2, cr2lt, p2 (p2), [k8, p2, cr2rt, p2, k3, p2, cr2lt, p2] 5 (6) times, nil (k8, p2). **2nd row:** K2, p2, k2, p3, k2, p2, k2 (k2), [p8, k2, p2, k2, p3, k2, p2, k2] 5 (6) times, nil (p8, k2). **3rd row:** P2, cr2lt, p2, k1, mb, k1, p2, cr2rt, p2 (p2), [c4b, c4f, p2, cr2lt, p2, k1, mb, k1, p2, cr2rt, p2] 5 (6) times, nil (c4b, c4f, p2).
4th row: As 2nd row. **5th row:** As 1st row.
6th row: As 2nd row. **7th row:** P2, cr2lt, p2, k1, mb, k1, p2, cr2rt, p2 (p2), [c4f, c4b, p2, cr2lt, p2, k1, mb, k1, p2, cr2rt, p2] 5 (6) times, nil (c4f, c4b, p2). **8th row:** As 2nd row.
These 8 rows form a repeat of the pattern. Pattern a further 114 rows. Mark each end of the last row for end of side seams. Pattern a further 78 (80) rows.
FOR SHOULDERS: Cast off 21 (25) sts at the beginning of each of the next 4 rows. Leave remaining 46 (50) sts on a spare needle.

FRONT

With No. 10 (3¼ mm) needles cast on 110 (122) sts and work as for back to **.
Change to No. 8 (4 mm) needles.

1st row: P2, cr2rt, p2, k3, p2, cr2lt, p2 (p2), [k8, p2, cr2rt, p2, k3, p2, cr2lt, p2] 5 (6) times, nil (k8, p2). **2nd row:** K2, p2, k2, p3, k2, p2, k2 (k2), [p8, k2, p2, k2, p3, k2, p2, k2] 5 (6) times, nil (p8, k2). **3rd row:** P2, cr2lt, p2, k1, mb, k1, p2, cr2rt, p2 (p2), [c4b, c4f, p2, cr2lt, p2, k1, mb, k1, p2, cr2rt, p2] 5 (6) times, nil (c4b, c4f, p2). **4th row:** As 2nd row.
5th row: As 1st row. **6th row:** As 2nd row.
7th row: P2, cr2lt, p2, k1, mb, k1, p2, cr2rt, p2 (p2), [c4f, c4b, p2, cr2lt, p2, k1, mb, k1, p2, cr2rt, p2] 5 (6) times, nil (c4f, c4b, p2).
8th row: As 2nd row.
These 8 rows form a repeat of the pattern. Pattern a further 114 rows. Mark each end of the last row for end of side seams. Pattern a further 53 (55) rows.
DIVIDE STS FOR FRONT NECK: Next row: Pattern 53 (61) and leave these sts on a spare needle for right front neck, pattern the next 24 (28) and leave these sts on a st holder, pattern to end and work on remaining 53 (61) sts for left front neck.
LEFT FRONT NECK: Dec 1 st at neck edge on each of the next 7 rows and then on the 4 following alternate rows – 42 (50) sts. Pattern a further 9 rows.
FOR SHOULDER: Cast off 21 (25) sts at beginning of the next row – 21 (25) sts. Pattern 1 row. Cast off.
RIGHT FRONT NECK: With right side of work facing, rejoin yarn to inner end of sts on spare needle. Dec 1 st at neck edge on each of the next 7 rows and then on the 4 following alternate rows – 42 (50) sts. Pattern a further 10 rows.
FOR SHOULDER: Cast off 21 (25) sts at beginning of the next row – 21 (25) sts. Pattern 1 row. Cast off.

SLEEVES

With No. 10 (3¼ mm) needles cast on 50 (54) sts and work 9 rows in twisted rib as given for back.

8

Increase row: Rib 3 (5), inc, [rib1, inc] to last 4 (6) sts, rib to end – 72 (76) sts. Change to No. 8 (4 mm) needles. **1st row:** P nil (2), k3, p2, cr2lt, p2, [k8, p2, cr2rt, p2, k3, p2, cr2lt, p2] twice, k8, p2, cr2rt, p2, k3, p nil (2). **2nd row:** K nil (2), p3, k2, p2, k2, [p8, k2, p2, k2, p3, k2, p2, k2] twice, p8, k2, p2, k2, p3, k nil (2). **3rd row:** P nil (2), k1, mb, k1, p2, cr2rt, p2, [c4b, c4f, p2, cr2lt, p2, k1, mb, k1, p2, cr2rt, p2] twice, c4b, c4f, p2, cr2lt, p2, k1, mb, k1, p nil (2). **4th row:** As 2nd row.

These 4 rows set the position of the pattern for the sleeves. Keeping continuity of pattern to match back and taking extra sts into pattern as they occur, inc 1 st at each end of the next row and the 25 following 4th rows – 124 (128) sts. Pattern a further 23 rows. Cast off.

NECKBAND

Join right shoulder seam. With right side of work facing and using No. 10 (3¼ mm) needles, pick up and k24 sts down left front neck, k across the 24 (28) sts at centre front, pick up and k24 sts up right front neck, then k across the 46 (50) sts at back neck – 118 (126) sts. Beginning with the 2nd rib row, work 9 rows in rib as given for back. Cast off in rib.

TO MAKE UP

Press as given on ball band. Join left shoulder seam, continuing seam across neckband. Sew cast-off edge of sleeves between markers on back and front. Join sleeve and side seams.

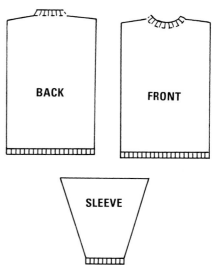

BACK   FRONT

SLEEVE

INSTANT
IMPACT

BE BOLD IN STRIKING CONTRAST STRIPES

MEASUREMENTS To fit bust sizes 86 (91-97) (102) (107-112) cm/34 (36-38) (40) (42-44) in.

Actual measurement 110.5 (117.5) (124.5) (131.5) cm/43½ (46¼) (49) (51¾) in. **Side seam** All sizes 39.5 cm/15½ in.

Length All sizes 65 cm/25½ in. **Sleeve seam** All sizes 38 cm/15 in.

MATERIALS

10 (11) (11) (12) 50 g balls of Patons Laguna D.K. in Navy (2027) and 6 (7) (7) (8) balls in Ecru (2022); No. 7 (4½ mm) and No. 9 (3¾ mm) knitting needles.
For stockists, write to Coats Patons Crafts, Customer Services, McMullen Road, Darlington, Co. Durham DL1 1YQ.

TENSION

17 stitches and 44 rows, to 10 x 10 cm/4 x 4 in, over the fancy rib pattern, slightly stretched, using No. 7 (4½ mm) needles.

NOTE

Instructions are given for 86 cm/34 in bust size. Where they vary, work figures in round brackets for larger sizes. Work instructions in square brackets as stated after 2nd bracket.

The easy pattern in this casual sweater is fisherman rib with a narrow, reverse stocking-stitch roll at the neck. The garment features dropped shoulders and a round neck. The yarn is machine-washable, pure cotton D.K.

BACK

With No. 9 (3¾ mm) needles and Navy cast on 94 (100) (106) (112) sts and work the fancy rib pattern as follows: **Foundation row:** K1, [yf, sl1 pwise, yon, k1] to last st, k1 more. **Pattern row:** K1, [yf, sl1 pwise, yon, k the yon of previous row and the next st tog] to last st, k1. Repeat the pattern row a further 12 times.

Change to No. 7 (4½ mm) needles. Pattern a further 48 rows. Break off Navy, then join in Ecru. Work the 112-row striped sequence as follows: With Ecru, pattern 56 rows. Break off Ecru, then rejoin Navy. With Navy, pattern 56 rows. These 112 rows form a repeat of the striped sequence. Mark each end of the last row, to denote end of side seams. Maintaining continuity of the striped sequence, pattern a further 112 rows. Cast off in pattern for shoulders and back neck, knitting the yon of previous row and next st tog as you cast off.

FRONT

With No. 9 (3¾ mm) needles and Navy cast on 94 (100) (106) (112) sts and work the fancy rib pattern as follows: **Foundation row:** K1, [yf, sl1 pwise, yon, k1] to last st, k1 more. **Pattern row:** K1, [yf, sl1 pwise, yon, k the yon of previous row and the next st tog] to last st, k1. Repeat the pattern row a further 12 times.

Change to No. 7 (4½ mm) needles. Pattern a further 48 rows. Break off Navy, then join in Ecru. Work the 112-row striped sequence as follows: With Ecru, pattern 56 rows. Break off Ecru, then rejoin Navy. With Navy, pattern 56 rows.

These 112 rows form a repeat of the striped sequence. Mark each end of the last row, to denote end of side seams. Maintaining continuity of the striped sequence, pattern a further 99 rows.

DIVIDE STS FOR FRONT NECK: Next row: Pattern 36 (38) (40) (42) and leave these sts on a spare needle for right front neck, cast off the next 22 (24) (26) (28) sts, pattern to end and work on remaining 36 (38) (40) (42) sts for left front neck.

LEFT FRONT NECK: Dec 1 st at neck edge on the next row and the 5 following alternate rows – 30 (32) (34) (36) sts. Pattern 1 row. Cast off in pattern for left front shoulder, knitting the yon of previous row and the next st tog as you cast off.

RIGHT FRONT NECK: With right side of work facing, rejoin Navy to inner end of sts on spare needle. Dec 1 st at neck edge on the next row and the 5 following alternate rows - 30 (32) (34) (36) sts. Pattern 1 row. Cast off in pattern for right front shoulder, knitting the yon of previous row and the next st tog as you cast off.

SLEEVES

With No. 9 (3¾ mm) needles and Navy cast on 44 sts and work the fancy rib pattern as follows: **Foundation row:** K1, [yf, sl1 pwise, yon, k1] to last st, k1 more. **Pattern row:** K1, [yf, sl1 pwise, yon, k the yon of previous row and the next st tog] to last st, k1. Repeat the pattern row a further 12 times. Change to No. 7 (4½ mm) needles. Pattern a further 4 rows. Maintaining continuity of the pattern and taking extra sts into the pattern as they occur, inc 1 st at each end of the next row and the 6 following 6th rows - 58 sts. Pattern 1 row.

Break off Navy, then join in Ecru. With Ecru, pattern 4 rows. Continuing with Ecru, inc 1 st at each end of the next row and the 8 following 6th rows – 76 sts. With Ecru, pattern a further 3 rows. Break off Ecru, then rejoin Navy. With Navy, pattern 2 rows, then inc 1 st at each end of the next row and the 4 following 6th rows – 86 sts. Pattern a further 29 rows. Cast off in pattern for sleeve top, knitting the yon of previous row and the next st tog as you cast off.

NECK EDGING

First sew 30 (32) (34) (36) sts cast off at right back neck to 30 (32) (34) (36) sts cast off at right front for shoulder. With right side of work facing and using No. 9 (3¾ mm) needles and Navy, pick up and k14 sts down shaped row-ends of left front neck, 24 (26) (28) (30) sts across sts cast off at centre front neck, 14 sts up shaped row-ends of right front neck, then 36 (38) (40) (42) sts across sts cast off at centre back neck, leaving 30 (32) (34) (36) sts at end free for shoulder – 88 (92) (96) (100) sts. Beginning with a p row, ss 2 rows. Cast off pwise.

TO MAKE UP

Do not press. Join left shoulder seam, continuing seam across neck edging. Sew cast-off edge of sleeves to row-ends between markers on back and front. Join sleeve and side seams, taking care to match stripes.

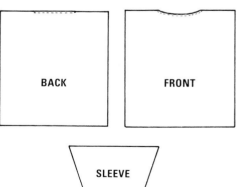

PALE
PERFECTION

A BEAUTIFULLY STYLED CASUAL JERSEY TO WEAR WITH FLAIR

MEASUREMENTS To fit sizes 86-91 (97) (102) cm/34-36 (38) (40) in.

Actual measurement 107 (111.5) (115.5) cm/42 (43¾) (45½) in. **Side seam** All sizes 40 cm/15¾ in.

Length All sizes 62.5 cm/24½ in. **Sleeve seam** All sizes 41.5 cm/16¼ in.

MATERIALS

15 (15) (16) 50 g balls of Sirdar Soft Cotton D.K.; No. 8 (4 mm) and No. 10 (3¼ mm) knitting needles; a cable needle. Yarn: used Blue Dolphin (645).
For stockists, write to Sirdar plc, Flanshaw Lane, Alverthorpe, Wakefield, West Yorkshire WF2 9ND.

TENSION

28 stitches and 31 rows, to 10 x 10 cm/4 x 4 in, over pattern, using No. 8 (4 mm) needles.

NOTE

Instructions are given for 86-91 cm/34-36 in size. Where they vary, work figures in round brackets for larger sizes. Work instructions in square brackets as stated after 2nd bracket.

Shallow set-in sleeves and a wide round neck are the basic design features of this sweater. The pattern is reverse stocking stitch, with cable and twist diamond panels, and the yarn is machine-washable, pure soft cotton D.K.

BACK

With No. 10 (3¼ mm) needles cast on 110 (116) (122) sts and single rib 19 rows.
Increase row: K8 (11) (14), * [inc pwise] 4 times, k3, ** [inc pwise] twice, k3, inc kwise, k3 **; work from ** to ** once more, [inc pwise] twice, k3 *; work from * to * twice more, [inc pwise] 4 times, k8 (11) (14) – 150 (156) (162) sts. Change to No. 8 (4 mm) needles. Work 48-row pattern thus:
1st row: For rss, p8 (11) (14), * for cable panel k8, for diamond panel p3, [c4b, p8] twice, c4b, p3; work from * twice more, for cable panel k8, for rss, p8 (11) (14). **2nd and every alternate row:** K and p to end with sts as set. **3rd row:** Rss 8 (11) (14), * for cable c4b, c4f, for diamond p3, [k4, p8] twice, k4, p3; work from * twice more, for cable c4b, c4f, rss to end. **4th row:** Rss 8 (11) (14), * for cable p8, for diamond k3, [p4, k8] twice, p4, k3; work from * twice more, for cable p8, rss to end. These 4 rows form a repeat of the cable. Keeping cable panel correct, work thus: **5th to 10th rows:** Repeat 1st to 4th rows, once more, then 1st and 2nd rows again. **11th row:** Rss 8 (11) (14), * cable 8, for diamond p5, [cr4lt, p4, cr4rt] twice, p5; work from * twice more, cable 8, rss to end. **13th row:** Rss 8 (11) (14), * cable 8, for diamond p7, [tw2, p4] 3 times, tw2, p7; work from * twice more, cable 8, rss to end.
15th to 22nd rows Repeat 13th and 14th rows, 4 times more. **23rd row:** Rss 8 (11) (14), * cable 8, for diamond p7, cr4lt, cr4rt, p4, cr4lt, cr4rt, p7; work from * twice more, cable 8, rss to end. **25th row:** Rss 8 (11) (14), * cable 8, for diamond p9, c4b, p8, c4b, p9; work

from * twice more, cable 8, rss to end. **27th row:** Rss 8 (11) (14), * cable 8, for diamond p9, k4, p8, k4, p9; work from * twice more, cable 8, rss to end. **29th to 34th rows:** Repeat 25th to 28th rows, once more, then 25th and 26th rows again. **35th row:** Rss 8 (11) (14), * cable 8, for diamond p7, cr4rt, cr4lt, p4, cr4rt, cr4lt, p7; work from * twice more, cable 8, rss to end. **37th to 46th rows:** Repeat 13th to 22nd rows. **47th row:** Rss 8 (11) (14), * cable 8, for diamond p5, [cr4rt, p4, cr4lt] twice, p5; work from * twice more, cable 8, rss to end. **48th row:** Rss 8 (11) (14), * cable 8, for diamond k3, p4, k8, p4, k8, p4, k3; work from * twice more, cable 8, rss to end. Pattern another 56 rows.
TO SHAPE ARMHOLES: Cast off 2 sts at beginning of next 2 rows, then dec 1 st at beginning only of next 8 rows – 138 (144) (150) sts. *** Pattern another 60 rows.
FOR SHOULDERS: Cast off 39 (41) (43) sts at beginning of next 2 rows. Leave 60 (62) (64) sts on a spare needle.

FRONT

Work as given for back to ***. Pattern another 41 rows.
DIVIDE STS FOR FRONT NECK: Next row: Pattern 55 (57) (59) and leave these sts on a spare needle for right front neck, pattern next 28 (30) (32) sts and leave them on a st holder, pattern to end and work on these 55 (57) (59) sts for left front neck.
LEFT FRONT NECK: Pattern 1 row – omit this row here when working right front neck. Cast off 3 sts at beginning of next row and 2 following alternate rows, then 2 sts on next 2 alternate rows.
Pattern 1 row here for right front neck. Dec 1 st at neck edge on next row and 2 following alternate rows – 39 (41) (43) sts. Pattern 3 rows – pattern 4 rows here for right front neck. Cast off for shoulder.
RIGHT FRONT NECK: With right side of work facing, rejoin yarn to inner end of sts on spare

needle and work as given for left front neck to end, noting variations.

SLEEVES

With No. 10 (3¼ mm) needles cast on 48 (50) (52) sts and single rib 13 rows.
Increase row: K7 (8) (9), [inc pwise] 4 times, k3, * [inc pwise] twice, k3, inc kwise, k3; work from * once more, [inc pwise] twice, k3, [inc pwise] 4 times, k7 (8) (9) – 64 (66) (68) sts. Change to No. 8 (4 mm) needles.
1st row: For rss, p7 (8) (9), for cable k8, for diamond p3, [c4b, p8] twice, c4b, p3, for cable k8, for rss, p7 (8) (9). **2nd row:** For rss, k7 (8) (9), for cable p8, for diamond k3, [p4, k8] twice, p4, k3, for cable p8, for rss k7 (8) (9). These 2 rows place pattern for sleeves. Keeping continuity of cable and diamond panels to match back, working extra sts in rss as they occur, inc 1 st each end of next row and 28 (27) (26) following 3rd rows – 122 sts. Pattern a another 27 (30) (33) rows.
TO SHAPE SLEEVE TOP: Cast off 2 sts at beginning of next 2 rows, then dec 1 st at beginning of next 8 rows – 110 sts. Cast off.

NECKBAND

Join right shoulder seam. With right side facing and using No. 10 (3¼ mm) needles, pick up and k24 sts down left front neck edge, k across 28 (30) (32) sts at centre front, pick up and k24 sts up right front neck edge, then k across 60 (62) (64) sts at back neck – 136 (140) (144) sts. Single rib 8 rows. Cast off in rib.

TO MAKE UP

Press as given on ball band. Join left shoulder seam, including neckband. Set sleeves into armholes, then join sleeve and side seams.

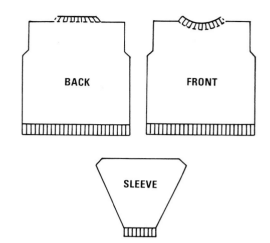

BACK FRONT

WOMEN

SLEEVE

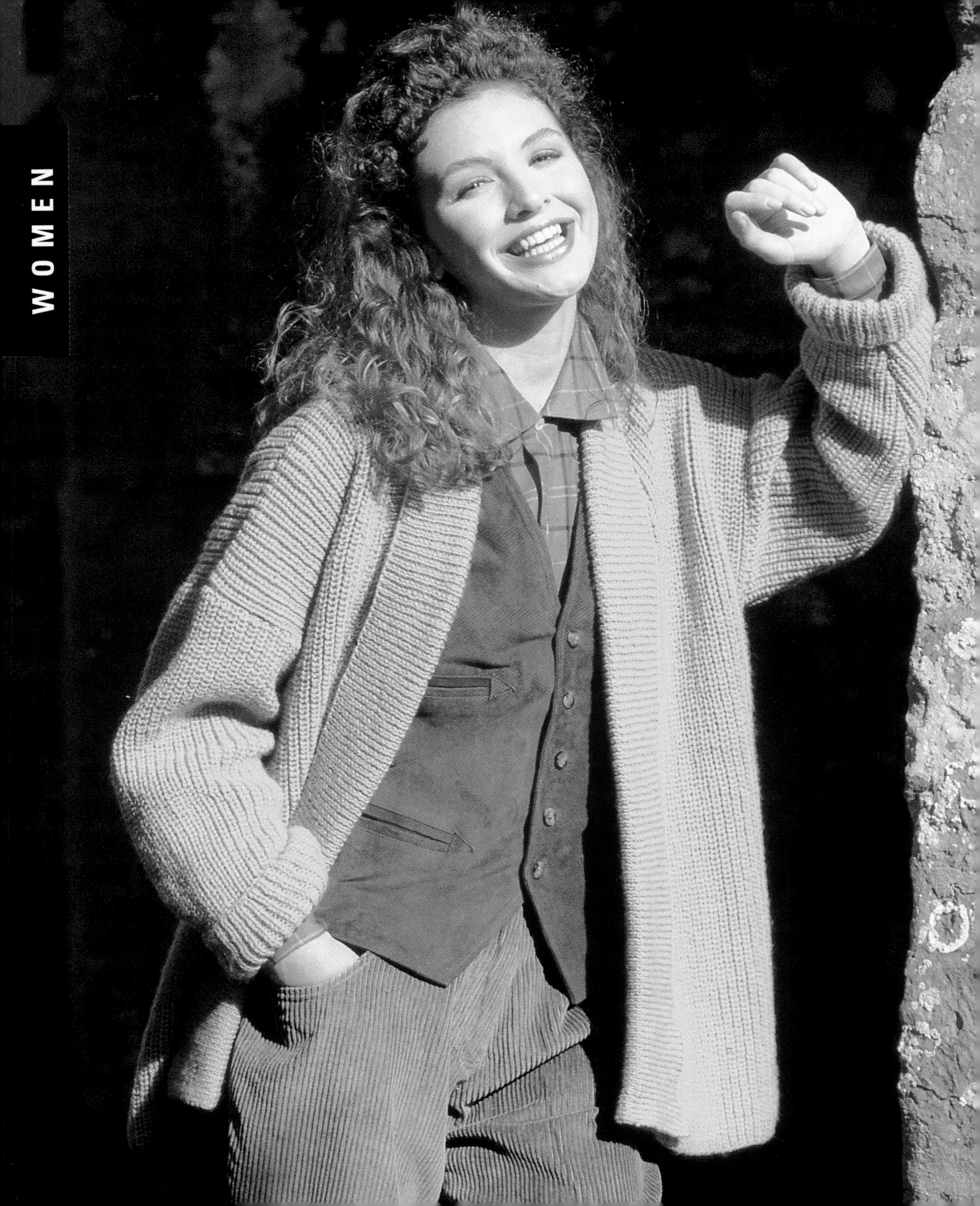

Golden Glow

STAY WARM AND STYLISH IN THIS COSY KNITTED JACKET

MEASUREMENTS To fit loosely, sizes 84 (91) (97) cm/34 (36) (38) in.

Actual measurement Edge to edge 123 (127.5) (134) cm/48¼ (50¼) (52¾) in.

Side seam All sizes 44 cm/17¼ in. **Length** 68.5 (69.5) (70.5) cm/27 (27¼) (27¾) in.

Sleeve seam All sizes, with cuff turned back 38.5 cm/15 in.

MATERIALS

8 (8) (9) 100 g balls of Sunbeam Swallow D.K.; No. 8 (4 mm) and No. 10 (3¼ mm) knitting needles; a No. 10 (3¼ mm) circular knitting needle. Yarn used: Mustard (511).
For stockists, write to Thomas B. Ramsden and Co Ltd, Westgate Common Mills, Alverthorpe Road, Wakefield, West Yorkshire WF2 9NR.

TENSION

23 stitches and 44 rows to 10 x 10 cm/4 x 4 in, over fisherman rib, using No. 8 (4 mm) needles.

NOTE

Instructions are given for the 86 cm /34 in size. Where they vary, work figures within rounded brackets for larger sizes. Work directions in square brackets as stated after 2nd bracket.

This generous edge-to-edge jacket has dropped shoulders, turn-back cuffs, and a shawl collar and front band. It is knitted mainly in fisherman rib, with a single-rib front band. The yarn is machine-washable, acrylic/bri-nylon wool D.K.

BACK

With No. 10 (3¼ mm) needles cast on 129 (135) (141) sts.
Change to No. 8 (4 mm) needles and work 2-row fisherman rib pattern thus: **1st row (right side):** Sl1, k to end. **2nd row:** Sl1, k1b, [p1, k1b] to last st, k1.
These 2 rows form a repeat of the fisherman rib pattern for the back. Pattern another 192 rows. Mark each end of last row, to denote end of side seams. Pattern another 106 (110) (114) rows.
FOR SHOULDERS: Cast off fairly loosely, 41 (43) (45) sts at beginning of each of the next 2 rows. Break yarn and leave remaining 47 (49) (51) sts on a spare needle.

LEFT FRONT

With No. 10 (3¼ mm) needles cast on 59 (61) (65) sts.
Change to No. 8 (4 mm) needles, and work the 2-row fisherman rib pattern thus: **1st row (right side):** Sl1, k to end. **2nd row:** Sl1, k1b, [p1, k1b] to last st, k1.
These 2 rows form a repeat of the fisherman rib for the left front. Pattern another 186 rows.
SHAPE FRONT EDGE: Keeping continuity of pattern, dec 1 st at end – front edge – of next row – 58 (60) (64) sts. Pattern 5 rows. Mark end of last row, to denote end of side seam. Dec 1 st at end of next row, and at same edge the 16 (16) (18) following 6th rows – 41 (43) (45) sts. Pattern 9 (13) (5) rows. Cast off fairly loosely, for shoulder.

RIGHT FRONT

With No. 10 (3¼ mm) needles cast on 59 (61) (65) sts.
Change to No. 8 (4 mm) needles and work the 2-row fisherman rib pattern thus: **1st row (right side):** Sl1, k to end. **2nd row:** Sl1, k1b, [p1, k1b] to last st, k1.
These 2 rows form a repeat of the fisherman rib pattern for the right front. Pattern another 186 rows.
SHAPE FRONT EDGE: Dec 1 st at beginning of next row – 58 (60) (64) sts. Pattern 5 rows. Mark beginning of last row, to denote end of side seam. Dec 1 st at beginning of next row, and at same edge on the 16 (16) (18) following 6th rows – 41 (43) (45) sts. Pattern another 10 (14) (6) rows. Cast off fairly loosely, for shoulder.

SLEEVES

With No. 10 (3¼ mm) needles cast on 65 (67) (71) sts.
Change to No. 8 (4 mm) needles and work 2-row fisherman rib pattern thus: **1st row (right side):** Sl1, k to end. **2nd row:** Sl1, k1b, [p1, k1b] to last st, k1.
These 2 rows form a repeat of the fisherman rib pattern for the sleeves. Pattern another 24 rows. Keeping continuity of pattern, and working extra sts into pattern as they occur, inc 1 st each end of the next row, and the 22 (23) (23) following 7th rows – 111 (115) (119) sts. Pattern another 11 (4) (4) rows. Cast off fairly loosely.

FRONT BAND

Join shoulder seams. With right side of work facing, rejoin yarn to lower edge, and using No. 10 (3¼ mm) circular knitting needle, pick up and k148 sts from straight row-ends of right front edge to first front shaping, pick up and k 94 (97) (100) sts from shaped row-ends to shoulder, work across back neck sts thus: k5 (6) (7), inc, [k8, inc] 4 times, k5 (6) (7), pick up and k94 (97) (100) sts from shaped row ends of left front, down to first front shaping row, and finally, pick up and k148 sts from straight row-ends down to cast-on edge – 536 (544) (552) sts. Working backwards and forwards in rows, work 59 rows in single rib. Cast off fairly loosely in rib.

TO MAKE UP

Press as given on ball band. Sew sts cast off at top of sleeves, to row-ends between markers on back and fronts. Join side and sleeve seams, reversing seams for 5 cm/2 in at cuff edge for turn back. Turn cuff to right side. Fold front band in half to right side.

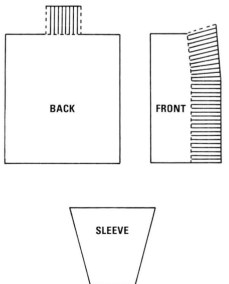

BACK

FRONT

SLEEVE

STYLISH WAISTCOAT

COMFORT AND ELEGANCE IN A CLASSIC CABLE KNIT WAISTCOAST

MEASUREMENTS **To fit sizes** 81-86 (91-97) (102-107) cm/32-34 (36-38) (40-42) in.

Actual measurement 103 (113) (123.5) cm/40½ (44½) (48½) in. **Side seam** All sizes 42.5 cm/16¾ in.

Length 67.5 (68) (69) cm/26½ (26¾) (27) in.

MATERIALS

6 (6) (7) 100 g balls of Littlewoods Soft Cotton Aran; No. 7 (4½ mm) and No. 9 (3¾ mm) knitting needles; a cable needle; 5 buttons. Yarn used: Cream.
For stockists, write to Andrea Wood, Littlewoods Chainstore Ltd, Atlantic Pavilion, Albert Dock, Liverpool L70 7AD.

TENSION

18 stitches and 25 rows, to 10 x 10 cm/4 x 4 in, over stocking stitch, 1 cable panel of 17 stitches, to measure 6.5 cm/2½ in in width and 1 ribbed panel of 11 stitches, to measure 4 cm in width, using No. 7 (4½ mm) needles.

NOTE

Instructions are given for 81-86 cm/32-34 in size. Where they vary, work figures in round brackets for larger sizes. Work instructions in square brackets as stated after the 2nd bracket.

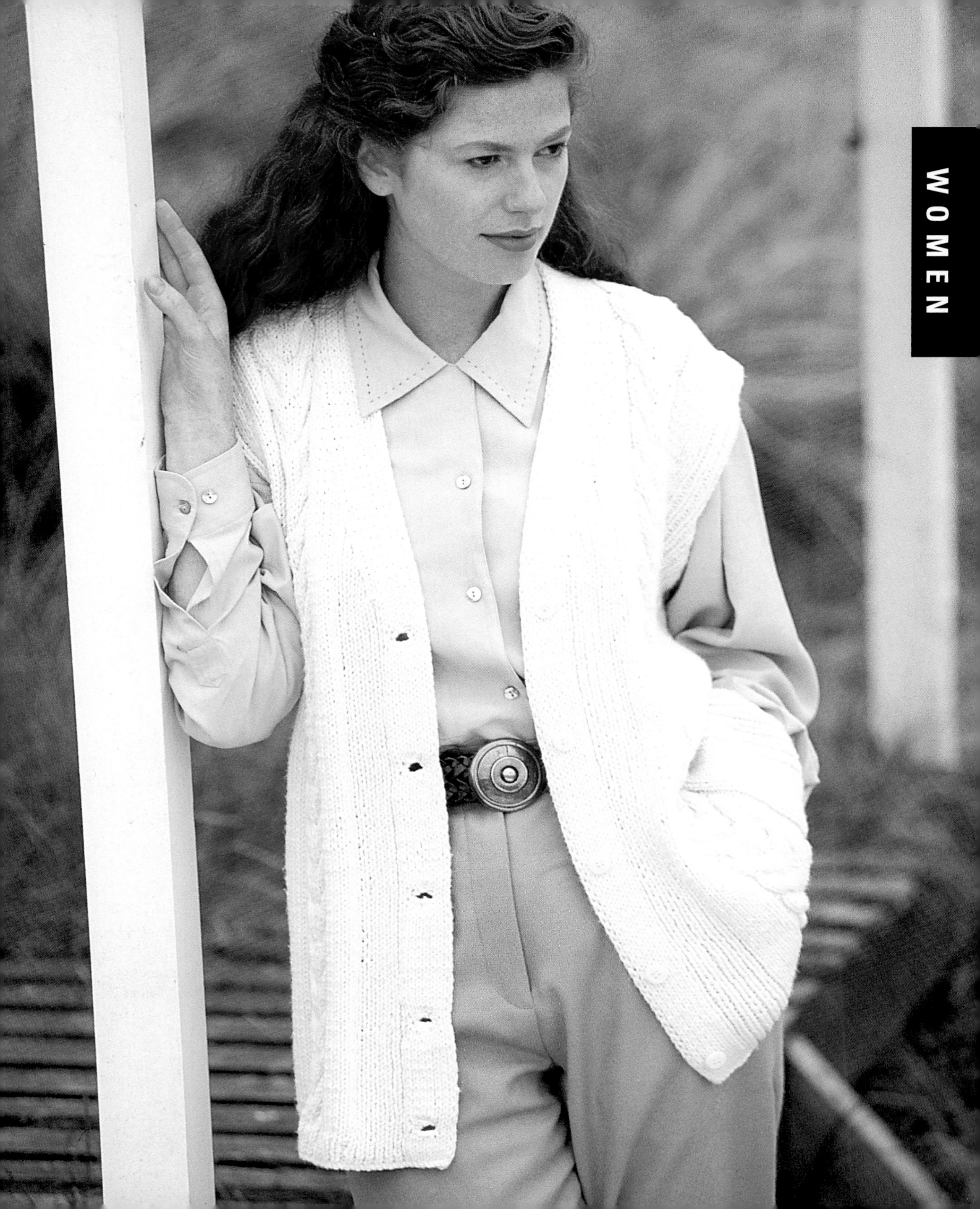

This attractive waistcoat has curved armholes, and buttons to a V-neck. The pattern consists of classic cable and rib panels, which are easy for the not very experienced knitter. It has a narrow lower ribbed border, and the stocking stitch front bands are knitted in with the fronts. The armhole hems are worked in stocking stitch and folded to the wrong side. The yarn is machine-washable, cotton/acrylic Aran weight.

BACK

With No. 9 (3¼ mm) needles cast on 117 (127) (137) sts and, beginning odd-numbered rows with k1 and even-numbered rows with p1, single rib 6 rows.
Change to No. 7 (4½ mm) needles and work the 8-row pattern thus: **1st row:** For ss panel k7, * for rib panel p1, [k1, p1] 5 times, for ss panel k5 (7) (9), for cable panel p2, k13, p2, for ss panel k5 (7) (9), for rib panel p1, [k1, p1] 5 times *, for ss panel k5 (7) (9), work from * to * once, for ss panel k7.
2nd and every alternate row: K and p to end with sts as set. **3rd to 6th rows:** Repeat 1st and 2nd rows, twice more. **7th row:** For ss panel k7, * for rib panel p1, [k1, p1] 5 times, for ss panel k5 (7) (9), for cable panel p2, c6b, k1, c6f, p2, for ss panel k5 (7) (9), for rib panel p1, [k1, p1] 5 times *, for ss panel k5 (7) (9), work from * to * once, for ss panel k7.
8th row: As 2nd row.
These 8 rows form the pattern. Pattern another 92 rows.
FOR ARMHOLES: Cast off 5 sts at beginning of next 2 rows, then dec 1 st at each end of the next row and the 5 (7) (9) following alternate rows – 95 (101) (107) sts. Pattern another 43 (41) (39) rows.
FOR SHOULDERS: Cast off 10 sts at beginning of next 2 rows, then 9 (10) (11) sts at begin-

ning of following 4 rows.
Cast off remaining 39 (41) (43) sts.

LEFT FRONT

With No. 9 (3¼ mm) needles cast on 71 (75) (81) sts and work thus: **1st row:** [K1, p1] to last 15 (15) (17) sts, k15 (15) (17) sts for front border. **2nd row:** P7 (7) (8), sl1, p7 (7) (8) for front border, then [k1, p1] to end. Repeat last 2 rows, twice more.
Change to No. 7 (4½ mm) needles. Place pattern thus: **1st row:** For ss panel k7, for rib panel p1, [k1, p1] 5 times, for ss panel k5 (7) (9), for cable panel p2, k13, p2, for ss panel k5 (7) (9), for rib panel p1, [k1, p1] 5 times, k15 (15) (17) for border. **2nd and alternate rows:** Keeping border correct, k and p to end with sts as set. These 2 rows place position of pattern for left front. Keeping continuity of front border and pattern to match back, pattern another 98 rows.
FOR ARMHOLE AND TO SHAPE FRONT EDGE: 1st row: Cast off 5 sts, pattern to last 17 (17) (19) sts, dec, k to end. **2nd row:** Pattern to end. **3rd row:** Dec, pattern to last 17 (17) (19) sts, dec, k to end. Repeat 2nd and 3rd rows, 5 times more – 53 (57) (63) sts.
FOR 2ND SIZE ONLY: 1st row: Pattern to end. **2nd row:** Dec, pattern to end. **3rd row:** As 1st row. **4th row:** Dec, pattern to last 17 sts, dec, pattern to end – 54 sts.
FOR 3RD SIZE ONLY:
1st row: Pattern to end. **2nd row:** Dec, pattern to end. **3rd row:** As 1st row. **4th row:** Dec, pattern to last 19 sts, dec, pattern to end. Repeat last 4 rows, once more – 57 sts.
FOR ALL SIZES: Pattern 3 rows, then dec 1 st at front edge only as before, on the next row and the 8 (7) (6) following 4th rows - 44 (46) (50) sts. Pattern 7 (9) (11) rows.
FOR SHOULDER: Cast off 10 sts at beginning of next row, then 9 (10) (11) sts on the 2 following alternate rows – 16 (16) (18) sts. Pattern 19 (21) (23) rows. Cast off.

RIGHT FRONT

With No. 9 (3¾ mm) needles cast on 71 (75) (81) sts. **1st row:** K15 (15) (17) sts for front border, [p1, k1] to end. **2nd row:** [P1, k1] to last 15 (15) (17) sts, p7 (7) (8), sl1, p7 (7) (8). Repeat last 2 rows, twice more. Change to No. 7 (4½ mm) needles and place pattern and work buttonholes thus: **1st (buttonhole) row:** K2, cast off 3, k a further 4 (4) (6), cast off 3, k1 more, for rib panel p1, [k1, p1] 5 times, for ss panel k5 (7) (9), for cable panel p2, k13, p2, for ss panel k5 (7) (9), for rib panel p1, [k1, p1] 5 times, for ss panel k7. **2nd (buttonhole) row:** K and p with sts as set until border sts remain, p2, turn, cast on 3 sts, turn, p2 (2) (3), sl1, p2 (2) (3), turn, cast on 3, turn, p2. Keeping continuity of front border and pattern to match back, pattern another 99 rows, making a double buttonhole as before on the 23rd and 24th, 47th and 48th, 71st and 72nd and 95th and 96th of these rows.
FOR ARMHOLE AND SHAPE FRONT EDGE: 1st row: 9 Cast off 5 sts, pattern to end. **2nd row:** K15 (15) (17), skpo, pattern to last 2 sts, dec. **3rd row:** Pattern to end. Repeat 2nd and 3rd rows, 5 (6) (6) times.
FOR 1ST SIZE ONLY: K15, skpo, pattern to end.
FOR 2ND SIZE ONLY: 1st row: Pattern to last 2 sts, dec. **2nd row:** Pattern to end. **3rd row:** Pattern 15, skpo, pattern to end.
FOR 3RD SIZE ONLY: 1st row: Pattern to last 2 sts, dec. **2nd row:** Pattern to end. **3rd row:** K17, skpo, pattern to last 2 sts, dec. **4th row:** As 2nd row. **5th row:** As 1st row. **6th row:** As 2nd row. **7th row:** K17, skpo, pattern to end.
FOR ALL SIZES: Pattern 3 rows, dec 1 st at front edge only as before, on next row and 8 (7) (6) following 4th rows — 44 (46) (50) sts. Pattern another 6 (8) (10) rows.
FOR SHOULDER: Work as for left front — 16 (16) (18) sts. Pattern 18 (20) (22) rows. Cast off.

ARMHOLE FACINGS

Join shoulder seams. With right side facing and using No. 9 (3¾ mm) needles, pick up and k84 (88) (92) sts round armhole edge. Beginning with a p row, ss 6 rows, increasing 1 st each end of every row — 96 (100) (104) sts. Cast off.

TO MAKE UP

Press as given on ball band. Join side seams and armhole facings. Turn facings to wrong side and sl st in place. Join cast-off edges of front borders tog, then sew to back neck. Fold border in half at sl st and sew down on the wrong side. Neaten double buttonholes. Add buttons.

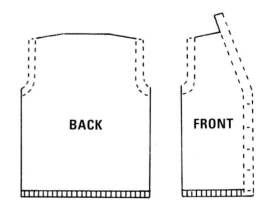

BACK   FRONT

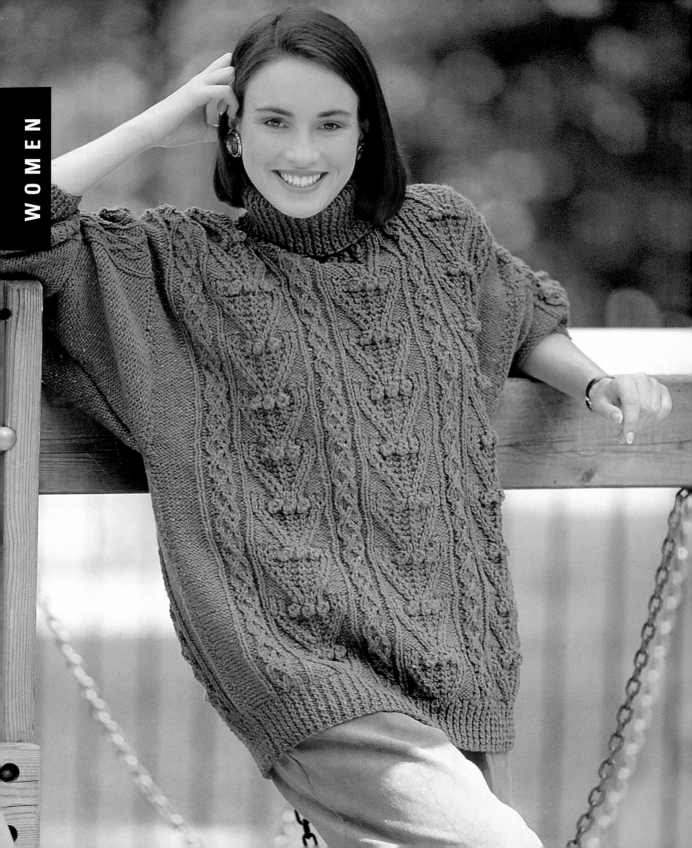

MELLOW
MOODS

WELCOME THE COLD SEASON WITH A COSY, CUDDLY SWEATER

MEASUREMENTS To fit bust sizes 86-91 (97) cm/34-36 (38) in. **Actual measurement** 117.5 (122) cm/46¼ (48) in.

Side seam both sizes 43 cm/17 in. **Length** both sizes 71 cm/28 in.

Sleeve seam both sizes 45.5 cm/18 in.

MATERIALS

For either size: Allow 22 50 g balls of tivoli Bainin Tweed. A pair each of No. 7 (4½ mm), No.8 (4 mm) and No. 9 (3¾ mm) knitting needles. Yarn used: shade 741.
For stockists, write to Tivoli, 28 Aulton Road, Sutton Coldfield, West Midlands B75 5PY.

TENSION

Work at a tension of 18 stitches and 24 rows, to measure 10 x 10 cm/4 x 4 in, over the reverse stocking stitch and centre 111 stitches to measure 51 cm (20 in), using No. 7 (4½ mm) needles.

NOTE

Instructions are given for 86-91 cm/34-36 in size. Where they vary, work figures in round brackets for larger size. Instructions in square brackets are worked as stated after 2nd bracket.

The dropped shoulders and polo collar make this an easy-fitting sweater. It is knitted in mainly reverse stocking stitch with bold twist and bobble panels on the back, front and sleeves. All borders and collar are worked in twisted rib. The yarn is pure wool Donegal Tweed, which knits to approximately Aran weight.

BACK

With No. 9 (3¾ mm) needles cast on 94 (98) sts and work in twisted single rib as follows: **Twisted rib row (right side):** [K1b, p1] to end. Repeat last row, 15 times more. **Increase row:** K2 (4), up1, [k3, up1] to last 2 (4) sts, k2 (4) – 125 (129) sts. Change to No. 7 (4½ mm) needles and work 16-row pattern as follows: **1st row (wrong side):** K7 (9), p1, k3, p5, k2, p1, [k7, p1, k1, p3, k1, p1, k7, p1, k3, p5, k2, p1] to last 7 (9) sts, k7 (9). **2nd row:** P7 (9), k1, p2, k3, tw2rt, p3, k1, [p6, cr4rt, k1b, cr4lt, p6, k1, p2, k3, tw2rt, p3, k1] to last 7 (9) sts, p7 (9). **3rd row:** K7 (9), p1, k3, p5, k2, p1, [k6, p1, k1, p1, k1, p1, k1, p1, k1, p1, k6, p1, k3, p5, k2, p1] to last 7 (9) sts, k7 (9). **4th row:** P7 (9), k1, p2, tw2lt, tw2rt, tw2lt, p2, k1, [p5, cr4rt, k1, k1b, k1, cr4lt, p5, k1, p2, tw2lt, tw2rt, tw2lt, p2, k1] to last 7 (9) sts, p7 (9). **5th row:** K7 (9), p1, k2, p5, k3, p1, [k5, p1, k1, p1, k2, p1, k2, p1, k1, p1, k5, p1, k2, p5, k3, p1] to last 7 (9) sts, k7 (9). **6th row:** P7 (9), k1, p3, tw2lt, k3, p2, k1, [p4, cr4rt, k2, k1b, k2, cr4lt, p4, k1, p3, tw2lt, k3, p2, k1] to last 7 (9) sts, p7 (9). **7th row:** K7 (9), p1, k2, p5, k3, p1, [k4, p1, k1, p2, k2, p1, k2, p2, k1, p1, k4, p1, k2, p5, k3, p1] to last 7 (9) sts, k7 (9). **8th row:** P7 (9), k1, p2, tw2rt, tw2lt, tw2rt, p2, k1, [p3, cr4rt, k1b, k2, k1b, k2, k1b, cr4lt, p3, k1, p2, tw2rt, tw2lt, tw2rt, p2, k1] to last 7 (9) sts, p7 (9). **9th row:** K7 (9), p1, k3, p5, k2, p1, [k3, p1, k1, p1, k1,

p1, k2, p1, k2, p1, k1, p1, k1, p1, k3, p1, k3, p5, k2, p1] to last 7 (9) sts, k7 (9). **10th row:** P7 (9), k1, p2, k3, tw2rt, p3, k1, [p2, cr4rt, k1, k1b, k2, k1b, k2, k1b, k1, cr4lt, p2, k1, p2, k3, tw2rt, p3, k1] to last 7 (9) sts, p7 (9). **11th row:** K7 (9), p1, k3, p5, k2, p1, [k2, p1, k1, p1, k2, p1, k2, p1, k2, p1, k2, p1, k1, p1, k2, p1, k3, p5, k2, p1] to last 7 (9) sts, k7 (9). **12th row:** P7 (9), k1, p2, tw2lt, tw2rt, tw2lt, p2, k1, [p1, cr4rt, k2, k1b, k2, k1b, k2, k1b, k2, cr4lt, p1, k1, p2, tw2lt, tw2rt, tw2lt, p2, k1] to last 7 (9) sts, p7 (9). **13th row:** K7 (9), p1, k2, p5, k3, p1, [k1, p1, k1, p1, k3, p1, k2, p1, k2, p1, k3, p1, k1, p1, k1, p1, k2, p5, k3, p1] to last 7 (9) sts, k7 (9). **14th row:** P7 (9), k1, p3, tw2lt, k3, p2, k1, [p1, k1b, p1, k1b, k3, mb, k2, mb, k2, mb, k3, k1b, p1, k1b, p1, k1, p3, tw2lt, k3, p2, k1] to last 7 (9) sts, p7 (9). **15th row:** K7 (9), p1, k2, p5, k3, p1, [k1, p1, k1, p1, k3, p1b, k2, p1b, k2, p1b, k3, p1, k1, p1, k1, p1, k2, p5, k3, p1] to last 7 (9) sts, k7 (9). **16th row:** P7 (9), k1, p2, tw2rt, tw2lt, tw2rt, p2, k1, [p1, k1b, p1, k1b, p3, k1b, p1, k1b, k1b, k1b, p1, k1b, p3, k1b, p1, k1b, p1, k1, p2, tw2rt, tw2lt, tw2rt, p2, k1] to last 7 (9) sts, p7 (9). Pattern a further 73 rows. Mark each end of last row, to denote end of side seams. ** Pattern a further 61 rows. **DIVIDE FOR BACK NECK: Next row:** Pattern 52 (54) and leave these sts on a spare needle for left back neck, pattern 21 and leave these sts on a st holder, pattern to end and work on remaining 52 (54) sts for right back neck. **RIGHT BACK NECK: 1st row:** Pattern to end. **2nd row:** Cast off 6 sts, pattern to end. **3rd row:** Pattern to last 2 sts, dec. **4th row:** Cast off 4 sts, pattern to end. **5th row:** Pattern to last 2 sts, dec. **6th row:** Pattern to end – 40 (42) sts. Cast off for shoulder. **LEFT BACK NECK:** With right side facing, rejoin yarn to inner end of sts on spare needle and continue as follows. **1st row:** Cast off 6 sts, pattern to end. **2nd row:** Pattern to last 2 sts, dec. **3rd row:** Cast off 4 sts, pattern to end. **4th row:** Pattern to last 2 sts, dec. **5th and 6th rows:** pattern to end. Cast off for shoulder.

FRONT

Work as given for back to **. Pattern a further 53 rows.

DIVIDE FOR NECK: Next row: Pattern 58 (60) and leave these sts on a spare needle for right front neck, pattern 9 and leave these sts on a st holder, pattern to end and work on remaining 58 (60) sts for left front neck.

LEFT FRONT NECK: 1st row: Pattern to end. **2nd row:** Cast off 5 sts, pattern to end. **3rd row:** Pattern to last 2 sts, dec. **4th row:** Cast off 2 sts, pattern to end. **5th to 8th rows:** Repeat 3rd and 4th rows, twice more. Dec 1 st at neck edge on next 4 rows – 40 (42) sts. Pattern 2 rows. Cast off for shoulder.

RIGHT FRONT NECK: With right side facing, rejoin yarn to inner end of sts on spare needle and continue as follows: **1st row:** Cast off 5 sts, pattern to end. **2nd row:** Pattern to last 2 sts, dec. **3rd row:** Cast off 2 sts, pattern to end. **4th to 7th rows:** Repeat 2nd and 3rd rows, twice more. **8th row:** Pattern to end. Dec 1 st at neck edge on next 4 rows – 40 (42) sts. Pattern 2 rows. Cast off for shoulder.

SLEEVES

With No. 9 (3¾ mm) needles cast on 40 sts and work 16 rows in twisted single rib as given for back. **Increase row:** [K2, up1] 9 times, k1, up1, k1, up1, k1, up1, k1. [up1, k2] 9 times – 61 sts.
Change to No. 7 (4½ mm) needles and work as follows: **1st row (wrong side):** K8, p1, k3, p5, k2, p1, k7, p1, k1, p3, k1, p1, k7, p1, k3, p5, k2, p1, k8. **2nd row:** P8, k1, p2, k3, tw2rt, p3, k1, p6, cr4rt, k1b, cr4lt, p6, k1, p2, k3, tw2rt, p3, k1, p8.
These 2 rows set position of pattern for the sleeves. Keeping continuity of pattern as set, taking extra sts into rss at each end as they occur continue thus: Inc 1 st at each end of the next 2 rows, then pattern 4 rows. Repeat last 6 rows, 11 times – 109 sts. Inc 1 st each end of next row – 111 sts. Pattern a further 20 rows. Cast off.

POLO COLLAR

Join right shoulder seam. With right side facing, using No. 9 (3¾ mm) needles, pick up and k18 sts down left front neck, k the 9 sts at centre front, pick up and k18 sts up right front neck, 15 down right back neck, k the 21 sts at centre back neck, then pick up and k15 sts up left back neck – 96 sts. Work 15 rows in twisted rib as for back.
Change to No. 8 (4 mm) needles. Rib a further 25 rows. Cast off loosely in rib.

TO MAKE UP

Press as given on ball band. Join left shoulder seam, continuing seam along polo collar, reversing seam to allow for fold back. Sew cast-off edge of sleeves to row-ends between markers on back and front. Join side and sleeve seams. Fold polo collar to right side.

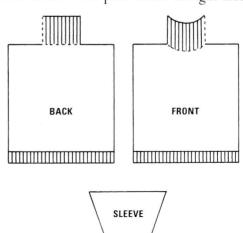

BACK   FRONT

SLEEVE

TOPS
FOR
TEXTURE

A RICHLY TEXTURED SWEATER THAT'S STRONG ON STYLE

MEASUREMENTS To fit bust sizes 86-91 (97-102) cm/34-36 (38-40) in.

Actual measurement 120.5 (132.5) cm/47½ (52¼) in. **Side seam** Both sizes 47.5 cm/18¾ in.

Length Both sizes 77 cm/30¼in. **Sleeve seam** 44.5 cm/17½ in.

MATERIALS
21 50-g balls of Hayfield Raw Cotton Classics D.K.; No. 8 (4 mm) and No. 10 (3¼ mm) needles; a cable needle. Recommended yarn: White (001).
For stockists, write to Hayfield Textiles Ltd, Glusburn, Keighley, West Yorkshire BD20 8QP.

TENSION
27 stitches and 30 rows, to 10 x 10 cm / 4 x 4 in over berry stitch, and 28 stitches to 10 cm over pattern, using No. 8 (4 mm) needles.

NOTE
Instructions are for 86-91 cm/34-36 in size. Where they vary, work figures in round brackets for larger size. Work instructions in square brackets as stated after 2nd bracket.

The pattern in this longline sweater consists of intricately woven twist, bobble and cable panels, with blackberry stitch sides. The borders are twist rib with bobble cables running through. It has dropped shoulders and a stand-up neck. The yarn is machine-washable, cotton/acrylic D.K.

BACK

With No. 10 (3¼ mm) needles cast on 150 (166) sts. Work 8-row welt pattern thus:
1st row: [K2b, p2] 6 (8) times, * k5, [p2, k2b] 5 times, p2, k5 *, [p2, k2b] 9 times, p2, work * to *, [p2, k2b] 6 (8) times. **2nd and alternate rows:** [P2b, k2] 6 (8) times, * p5, [k2, p2b] 5 times, k2, p5 *, [k2, p2b] 9 times, k2, work * to *, [k2, p2b] to end. **3rd row:** [K2b, p2, tw2, p2] 3 (4) times, * cr5k, [p2, tw2, p2, k2b] twice, p2, tw2, p2, cr5k *, [p2, tw2, p2, k2b] 4 times, p2, tw2, p2, work * to *, [p2, tw2, p2, k2b] to end.
5th row: As 1st row. **7th row:** [K2b, p2, tw2, p2] 3 (4) times, * k2, mb, k2, [p2, tw2, p2, k2b] twice, p2, tw2, p2, k2, mb, k2 *, [p2, tw2, p2, k2b] 4 times, p2, tw2, p2, work * to *, [p2, tw2, p2, k2b] to end. **8th row:** As 2nd row. Pattern another 15 rows. **Increase row:** Pattern 10 (18), * up1, [pattern 2, up1] 5 times *, pattern 20, up1, pattern 28, up1, [pattern 7, up1] twice, pattern 28, up1, pattern 20, work * to *, pattern 10 (18) − 167 (183) sts.
Change to No. 8 (4 mm) needles.
WORK MAIN PATTERN THUS: 1st row: For berry st, p27 (35), ** for bobble panel k1b, p2, k5, p2, k1b *, for dmst panel, p4, mb, p1, k2, mb, k2, p1, mb, p4, work ** to *, then **, for centre panel p7, k2b, p1, k2b, p11, k2b, p1, k2b, p7, work ** to **, for berry st, p27 (35). **2nd row:** For berry st, k2, [3 from 1, k3tog] 6 (8) times, k1, ** for bobble p1b, k2, p5, k2, p1b *, for dmst, k6, p2b, k1,

p2b, k6, work ** to *, then **, for centre k7, p2b, k1, p2b, k11, p2b, k1, p2b, k7, work ** to **, for berry st, k2, [3 from 1, k3tog] 6 (8) times, k1. **3rd row:** For berry st, p27 (35), ** for bobble k1b, p2, cr5k, p2, k1b *, for dmst, p5, tw3b, k1, tw3f, p5, work ** to *, then **, for centre p7, cr5p, p5, mb, p5, cr5p, p7, work ** to **, for berry st, p to end. **4th row:** For berry st, k2, [k3tog, 3 from 1] 6 (8) times, k1, ** bobble as 2nd row, for dmst, k5, p2b, k1, p1, k1, p2b, k5, bobble as 2nd row **, for centre k7, p2b, k1, p2b, k11, p2b, k1, p2b, k7, work ** to **, for berry st, k2, [k3tog, 3 from 1] 6 (8) times, k1.
These 4 rows form berry st. Continue thus:
5th row: Berry 27 (35), ** bobble as 1st row, for dmst, p4, tw3b, k1, p1, k1, tw3f, p4, bobble as 1st row **, for centre p6, tw3b, p1, tw3f, p9, tw3b, p1, tw3f, p6, work ** to **, berry to end. **6th and every alternate row:** Berry 27 (35), k and p next 113 sts with sts as set, working p1 or 2b over k1 or 2b of previous row, berry to end. **7th row:** Berry 27 (35), ** for bobble k1b, p2, k2, mb, k2, p2, k1b *, for dmst, p3, tw3b, k1, p1, k1, p1, k1, tw3f, p3, work ** to *, then **, for centre p5, tw3b, p3, tw3f, p7, tw3b, p3, tw3f, p5, work ** to **, berry to end. **8th row:** As 6th row. These 8 rows form bobble panel. Continue thus: **9th row:** Berry 27 (35), ** pattern 11, for dmst, p2, tw3b, [k1, p1] 3 times, k1, tw3f, p2, pattern 11 **, for centre p4, tw3b, p5, tw3f, p5, tw3b, p5, tw3f, p4, work ** to **, berry to end. **11th row:** Berry 27 (35), ** pattern 11, for dmst, p1, tw3b, [k1, p1] 4 times, k1, tw3f, p1, pattern 11 **, for centre p3, tw3b, p7, tw3f, p3, tw3b, p7, tw3f, p3, work ** to **, berry to end. **13th row:** Berry 27 (35), ** pattern 11, for dmst, p1, k2b, [k1, p1] 5 times, k1, k2b, p1, pattern 11 **, for centre p2, tw3b, p9, tw3f, p1, tw3b, p9, tw3f, p2, work ** to **, berry to end. **14th row:** As 6th row. These 14 rows form dmst panel.
Continue thus: **15th row:** Pattern to centre

panel, p2, k2b, p5, mb, p5, cr5p, p5, mb, p5, k2b, p2, pattern to end. **17th row:** Pattern to panel, p2, tw3f, p9, tw3b, p1, tw3f, p9, tw3b, p2, pattern to end. **19th row:** Pattern to panel, p3, tw3f, p7, tw3b, p3, tw3f, p7, tw3b, p3, pattern to end. **21st row:** Pattern to panel, p4, tw3f, p5, tw3b, p5, tw3f, p5, tw3b, p4, pattern to end. **23rd row:** Pattern to panel, p5, tw3f, p3, tw3b, p7, tw3f, p3, tw3b, p5, pattern to end. **25th row:** Pattern to panel, p6, tw3f, p1, tw3b, p9, tw3f, p1, tw3b, p6, pattern to end. **26th row:** As 6th row. These 26 rows form centre panel. Keeping all panels correct, work another 96 rows. Mark each end of last row for side seams. Pattern another 86 rows.
FOR SHOULDERS: Cast off 57 (65) sts at beginning of next 2 rows. Leave 53 sts.

FRONT

Work as back to markers. Pattern 75 rows.
DIVIDE FOR NECK: Next row: Pattern 68 (76) and leave for right front neck, pattern 31 and leave on holder, pattern to end and work on these sts for left front neck.
LEFT FRONT NECK: Pattern 1 row – omit this row when working right front neck. Cast off 3 sts at beginning of next row and 2 alternate rows, then 2 sts on next alternate row – 57 (65) sts. Pattern 2 rows – pattern 3 rows here for right front neck. Cast off for shoulder.
RIGHT FRONT NECK: With right side facing, work as left front neck, noting variations.

SLEEVES

With No. 10 (3¼ mm) needles cast on 68 sts.
PLACE WELT: 1st row: P2, [k2b, p2] twice, k5, [p2, k2b] 9 times, p2, k5, [p2, k2b] twice, p2. Pattern 22 rows to match back. **Increase row:** Pattern 27, up1, [pattern 7, up1] twice, pattern 27 – 71 sts.

Change to No. 8 (4 mm) needles.
PLACE PATTERN: 1st row: For berry st, p7, working as 1st row of back, work 11 sts of bobble, 35 sts of centre, and 11 sts of bobble, for berry st, p7. Pattern 1 more row. Keeping panels correct to match back, inc each end of next row and 18 following 3rd rows, then 26 following alternate rows – 161 sts. Pattern 3 rows. Cast off.

NECKBAND

Join right shoulder. Using No. 10 (3¼ mm) needles, pick up and k21 down left front neck, work across centre front thus: [k2b, p2] twice, [k2togb, k1b, p2tog, p1] twice, k2togb, k1b, [p2, k2b] twice, pick up and k20 up right front neck, work across back neck thus: p1, k5, [p2, k2b] twice, p1, p2tog, k1b, k2togb, p2, k2b, p2, inc in next st, p2, k2b, p2, k2togb, k1b, p2tog, p1, [k2b, p2] twice, k5, inc in last st – 118 sts.
PLACE PATTERN: Next row: K2, p5, [k2, p2b] 9 times, k2, p5, k2, p2b, k2, p5, [k2, p2b] 11 times, k2, p5, k2, p2b, k2. Pattern 14 rows to match welt. Cast off in rib.

TO MAKE UP

Join left shoulder seam. Sew cast-off edge of sleeves to row-ends above markers. Join sleeve and side seams.

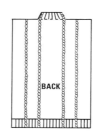
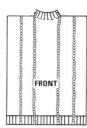

LACED
WITH
CREAM

FEEL EXTRA SPECIAL IN THIS STUNNING LACY SWEATER

MEASUREMENTS To fit bust sizes 86 (91) (97) cm/34 (36) (38) in.

Actual measurement 97 (104.5) (112) cm/38 (41¼) (44) in. **Side seam** All sizes 36.5 cm/14¼ in.

Length 62.5 (63) (64) cm/24½ (24¾) (25¼) in. **Sleeve seam** All sizes 40.5 cm/16 in.

MATERIALS

8 (9) (9) 100 g balls of Wendy Traditional Craft Cotton; No. 7 (4½mm) and No. 9 (3¾ mm) knitting needles; a No. 9 (3¾ mm) circular needle; a cable needle. Yarn used: Cream (181).
For stockists, write to Carter and Parker Ltd, Guiseley, West Yorkshire, LS20 9PD.

TENSION

22 stitches and 28 rows, to 10 x 10 cm/4 x 4 in, over pattern, using No. 7 (4½ mm) needles.

NOTE

Instructions are given for 86 cm/34 in size. Where they vary, work figures in round brackets for larger sizes. Work instructions in square brackets as stated after 2nd bracket.

This beautiful sweater has dropped shoulders and a round neck. The effective pattern is lacy and travelling bobble panels, and the borders and deep neck rib are lace and twist panels. The yarn is pure cotton which knits to Aran weight.

BACK

With No. 9 (3¾ mm) needles cast on 105 (116) (127) sts. Work 4-row welt pattern thus: **1st row:** P2, tw2lt, p2, [yon, skpo, k1, k2tog, yrn, p2, tw2lt, p2] to end. **2nd row:** K2, p2, k2, [p5, k2, p2, k2] to end. **3rd row:** P2, tw2lt, p2, [k1, yf, sl1, k2tog, psso, yf, k1, p2, tw2lt, p2] to end. **4th row:** As 2nd row. Repeat last 4 rows, 5 times, then 1st to 3rd rows again, increasing 2 sts (decreasing 1 st) (decreasing 4 sts) on last row – 107 (115) (123) sts. Change to No. 7 (4½ mm) needles. **Foundation (wrong side) row:** K1, [* for bobble panel k3 (4) (5), p1, k1, p1, k1, p2 *, k6 (7) (8), for lacy panel p15] to last 16 (18) (20) sts, work from * to *, k7 (8) (9). Work 20-row main pattern thus: **1st row:** P1, [* for bobble p5 (6) (7), cr2rt, cr2lt, cr2lt, cr2lt *, p2 (3) (4), for lacy k1, k2tog, k2tog, yf, k1, yf, k1, yf, k1, yf, skpo, skpo, k3] to last 16 (18) (20) sts, work from * to *, p3 (4) (5). **2nd and every following alternate row:** K and p to end with sts as set and working p1 over each made st and k1 over each mb. **3rd row:** P1, [* for bobble p5 (6) (7), k1, p2, cr2lt, cr2lt, cr2lt *, p1 (2) (3), for lacy k2tog, k2tog, yf, k1, yf, k3, yf, k1, yf, skpo, skpo, k2] to last 16 (18) (20) sts, work from * to *, p2 (3) (4). **5th row:** P1, [* for bobble p5 (6) (7), tw2lt, p2, cr2lt, cr2lt, mb *, p1 (2) (3), for lacy k3, k2tog, k2tog, yf, k1, yf, k1, yf, k1, yf, skpo, skpo, k1] to last 16 (18) (20) sts, work from * to *, p2 (3) (4). **7th row:** P1, [* for bobble p4 (5) (6), cr2rt, tw2lt, p2, cr2lt, mb *, p2 (3) (4), for lacy k2, k2tog, k2tog, yf, k1, yf, k3, yf, k1, yf,

skpo, skpo] to last 16 (18) (20) sts, work from * to *, p3 (4) (5). **8th row:** As 2nd row. These 8 rows form the lacy panel. Continue to work bobble panels thus: **9th row:** P1, [* for bobble p3 (4) (5), cr2rt, cr2rt, tw2lt, p2, mb *, p3 (4) (5), pattern 15] to last 16 (18) (20) sts, work from * to *, p4 (5) (6). **11th row:** P1, [* for bobble p2 (3) (4), cr2rt, cr2rt, cr2rt, cr2lt *, p5 (6) (7), pattern 15] to last 16 (18) (20) sts, work from * to *, p6 (7) (8). **13th row:** P1, [* for bobble p1 (2) (3), cr2rt, cr2rt, cr2rt, p2, k1 *, p5 (6) (7), pattern 15] to last 16 (18) (20) sts, work from * to *, p6 (7) (8). **15th row:** P1, [* for bobble p1 (2) (3), mb, cr2rt, cr2rt, p2, tw2rt *, p5 (6) (7), pattern 15] to last 16 (18) (20) sts, work from * to *, p6 (7) (8). **17th row:** P1, [* for bobble p2 (3) (4), mb, cr2rt, p2, tw2rt, cr2lt *, p4 (5) (6), pattern 15] to last 16 (18) (20) sts, work from * to *, p5 (6) (7). **19th row:** P1, [* for bobble p3 (4) (5), mb, p2, tw2rt, cr2lt, cr2lt *, p3 (4) (5), pattern 15] to last 16 (18) (20) sts, work from * to *, p4 (5) (6). **20th row:** As 2nd row. Pattern another 58 rows. Mark each end of last row for side seams. Pattern another 62 (64) (66) rows.
FOR SHOULDERS: Cast off 5 (7) (6) sts at beginning of next 2 rows, 6 sts on next 2 rows, then 6 (6) (7) sts on following 6 rows. Leave remaining 49 (53) (57) sts on a st holder.

FRONT

Work as back to markers. Pattern another 41 (43) (45) rows.
DIVIDE FOR FRONT NECK: Next row: Pattern 42 (44) (46) and leave these sts on a spare needle for right front neck, pattern 23 (27) (31) sts and leave on a st holder, pattern to end and work on these 42 (44) (46) sts for left front neck.
LEFT FRONT NECK: Dec 1 st at neck edge on next 9 rows, then 2 following alternate rows and then the 2 following 3rd rows – 29 (31) (33) sts.

Pattern 1 row – pattern 2 rows here when working right front neck.
FOR SHOULDER: Cast off 5 (7) (6) sts at beginning of next row, 6 sts on following alternate row, then 6 (6) (7) sts on next 2 alternate rows – 6 (6) (7) sts. Pattern 1 row. Cast off.
RIGHT FRONT NECK: With right side facing, rejoin yarn to sts on spare needle and work as left front neck, noting variation.

SLEEVES

With No. 9 (3¾ mm) needles cast on 39 sts, work 28 rows in welt pattern as back.
INCREASE (RIGHT SIDE) ROW: K1, [up1, inc] nil (3) (6) times(s), [up1, k1] to last nil (4) (7) sts, [up1, inc] nil (3) (6) time(s), nil (up1, k1) (up1, k1) – 77 (83) (89) sts.
Change to No. 7 (4½ mm) needles and work foundation row then 1st and 2nd main pattern rows of back. Keeping continuity of main pattern to match back and working extra sts in pattern as they occur, inc 1 st at each end of next row and 9 (7) (6) following 8th (10th) (12th) rows – 97 (99) (103) sts. Pattern 13 (15) (13) rows. Cast off.

NECKBAND

Join shoulder seams. With right side facing, using the No. 9 (3¾ mm) circular needle, sl first 24 (26) (28) sts at back neck on to a st holder, k remaining 25 (27) (29) sts, increasing 1 (2) (4) st(s), pick up and k30 sts down left front neck, k23 (27) (31) sts at centre front, increasing nil (2) (4) sts, pick up and k30 sts up right front neck, then k24 (26) (28) sts from st holder, increasing nil (2) (3) sts – 133 (146) (159) sts.
Work backwards and forwards in rows thus:
1st row: P4, [k3, p2, k3, p5] to last 12 sts, k3, p2, k3, p4. **2nd row:** K2, k2tog, yrn, p3, [tw2lt, p3, yon, skpo, k1, k2tog, yrn, p3] to last 9 sts, tw2lt, p3, yon, skpo, k2. **3rd row:**

As 1st row. **4th row:** K1, k2tog, yf, k1, p3, [tw2lt, p3, k1, yf, sl1, k2tog, psso, yf, k1, p3] to last 9 sts, tw2lt, p3, k1, yf, skpo, k1.
Repeat last 4 rows, twice more. **Next (dec) row:** P4, [k1, k2tog, p2, k1, k2tog, p5] to last 12 sts, k1, k2tog, p2, k1, k2tog, p4 – 113 (124) (135) sts. Keeping pattern correct, work another 11 rows. Cast off in pattern.

TO MAKE UP

Press as given on ball band. Sew cast-off edge of sleeves between markers on back and front. Join sleeve and side seams. Sew row-ends of neckband tog at centre back.

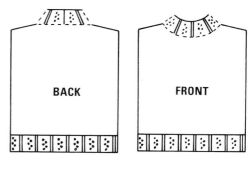

BACK   FRONT

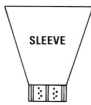

SLEEVE

NICE

AND

EASY

AN EASY-TO-KNIT, EVERY-DAY SWEATER THAT ALWAYS LOOKS GOOD

MEASUREMENTS To fit sizes 81-86 (91-97) (102) (107 cm/32-34 (36-38) (40) (42) in.

Actual measurement 117.5 (122.5) (127.5) (132.5) cm/46¼ (48¼) (50¼) (52¼) in. **Side seam** All sizes 44 cm/17¼ in.

Length 69.5 (70.5) (71.5) (72.5) cm/27¼ (27¾) (28) (28½) in. **Sleeve seam** All sizes 46 cm/18 in.

MATERIALS

11 (12) (13) (14) 50 g balls of Sirdar Balmoral D.K. in Charcoal (129) and 11 (12) (13) (14) balls in Cream (125); No. 4 (6 mm), No. 5 (5½ mm) and No. 6 (5 mm) knitting needles.
For stockists, write to Sirdar plc, Flanshaw Lane, Alverthorpe, Wakefield, West Yorkshire WF2 9ND. .

TENSION

16 stitches and 21 rows, to 10 x 10 cm/4 x 4 in, over the stocking stitch, using No. 4 (6 mm) knitting needles, and 1 strand of each colour together.

NOTE

Instructions are given for 81-86 cm 32-34 in size. Where they vary, work figures in round brackets for larger sizes. Work instructions in square brackets as stated after the 2nd bracket.

It is easy to make this loose-fitting sweater. It has dropped shoulders, a set-in breast pocket, and a wide fold-over collar. To give it a tweedy, chunky finish, it is knitted mainly in stocking stitch with wide rib borders and collar, using two strands of double knitting together. The yarn is wool/alpaca/silk D.K., which has a soft, silky feel.

WOMEN

BACK

With No. 6 (5 mm) needles and using 1 strand of each colour together throughout the garment, cast on 94 (98) (102) (106) sts. Work in double rib as follows: **1st rib row:** K2, [p2, k2] to end. **2nd rib row:** P2, [k2, p2] to end. Repeat the 2 rib rows, 4 times more. Change to No. 4 (6 mm) needles. Beginning with a k row, work 82 rows in ss. Mark each end of the last row, to denote end of side seams. Beginning with a k row, work a further 52 (54) (56) (58) rows in ss. **FOR SHOULDERS:** Cast off 29 (30) (31) (32) sts at the beginning of each of the next 2 rows. Leave remaining 36 (38) (40) (42) sts on a spare needle.

POCKET LINING

With No. 4 (6 mm) needles and 1 strand of each colour together, cast on 20 sts. Beginning with a k row, work 24 rows in ss. Leave sts on a st holder.

FRONT

With No. 6 (5 mm) needles and using 1 strand of each colour together, cast on 94 (98) (102) (106) sts. Work in double rib as follows: **1st rib row:** K2, [p2, k2] to end.

2nd rib row: P2, [k2, p2] to end. Repeat the 2 rib rows, 4 times more. Change to No. 4 (6 mm) needles. Beginning with a k row, work 82 rows in ss. Mark each end of the last row, to denote end of side seams. Beginning with a k row, work a further 6 rows in ss. **Next (pocket) row:** K24 (26) (28) (30) sts, slip next 20 sts on to a spare needle and leave at front of work, and in their place, k across the 20 sts of pocket lining, k to end of row. Beginning with a k row, work a further 26 (28) (30) (32) rows in ss.
DIVIDE STS FOR FRONT NECK: Next row: P39 (40) (41) (42) and leave these sts on a spare needle for right front neck, p the next 16 (18) (20) (22) and leave these sts on a st holder for polo collar, p to end and work on remaining 39 (40) (41) (42) sts for left front neck.
LEFT FRONT NECK: Dec 1 st at end – neck edge – of next row, and at same edge on the following 9 rows – 29 (30) (31) (32) sts. Beginning with a k row, work a further 8 rows in ss. Cast off for shoulder.
RIGHT FRONT NECK: With right side of work facing, rejoin 2 strands of yarn to inner end of sts on spare needle. Dec 1 st at beginning – neck edge – of next row, and at same end on the following 9 rows – 29 (30) (31) (32) sts. Beginning with a k row, work 9 rows in ss. Cast off for shoulder.

SLEEVES

With No. 6 (5 mm) needles and using 1 strand of each colour together, cast on 50 (54) (54) (58) sts and work in double rib as follows: **1st rib row:** K2, [p2, k2] to end. **2nd row:** P2, [k2, p2] to end. Repeat the 2 rib rows, 8 times more. Change to No. 4 (6 mm) needles. Beginning with a k row, work 4 rows in ss. Continuing in ss and taking extra sts into ss as they occur, inc 1 st at each end of the next row and the 15 (14) (15) (14) following 4th rows – 82 (84) (86) (88) sts. Beginning with a p row, work a further 13 (13) (17) (17) rows in ss. Cast off straight across for top of sleeve.

COLLAR

Join right shoulder seam. With right side of work facing and using No. 6 (5 mm) needles and 1 strand of each colour together, pick up and k22 sts down left front neck shaping, k across the 16 (18) (20) (22) sts at centre front, pick up and k22 sts up right front neck shaping, then finally, k across the 36 (38) (40) (42) sts left on spare needle at back neck – 96 (100) (104) (108) sts.
1st rib row: [K2, p2] to end. This row forms the double rib. Work a further 14 rows in double rib. Change to No. 5 (5½ mm) needles. **Increase row:** [K1, up1k, k1, p1, up1p, p1] to end – 144 (150) (156) (162) sts. **Next row:** [K3, p3] to end. Repeat the last row, 15 times more. Cast off in rib.

POCKET TOP

With right side of work facing and using No. 6 (5 mm) needles and 1 strand of each colour together, k across the 20 sts on spare needle, increasing 1 st at each end of the row – 22 sts. Beginning with the 2nd rib row, work 7 rows in double rib as given for back. Cast off in rib.

TO MAKE UP

Press as given on ball band. Join left shoulder seam, continuing seam across collar, and reversing seam for foldback. Sew cast-off edge of sleeves to row-ends above markers on back and front. Join sleeve and side seams. Sew down row-ends of pocket lining

on the wrong side and row-ends of pocket top on the right side. Fold collar in half to right side.

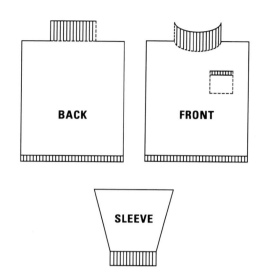

BACK FRONT

SLEEVE

SPLASH

OF

SCARLET

CUT A DASHING FIGURE IN THIS VIVID LONG-LINE CARDIGAN

MEASUREMENTS To fit sizes 81 (86) (91-97) (102-107) cm/32 (34) (36-38) (40-42) in.

Actual measurement 101 (109) (117) (125) cm/39¾ (42¾) (46) (49¼) in. **Side seam** All sizes 46 cm/18 in.

Length 70.5 (70.5) (70.5) (72) cm/27¾ (27¾) (27¾) (28¼) in. **Sleeve seam** All sizes 44.5 cm/17½ in.

MATERIALS

13 (15) (17) (19) 50 g balls of Sirdar Soft Cotton D.K. No. 8 (4 mm) and No. 10 (3¼ m) knitting needles; 5 buttons. Yarn used: Poppy Red (655).
For stockists, write to Sirdar plc, Flanshaw Lane, Alverthorpe, Wakefield, West Yorkshire WF2 9ND.

TENSION

25 stitches and 27 rows, to 10 x 10 cm/ 4 x 4 in, over pattern, using No. 8 (4 mm) needles.

NOTE

Instructions are given for 81 cm/32 in bust size. Where they vary, work figures in round brackets for larger sizes. Instructions in square brackets are worked as stated after 2nd bracket.

This stylish cardigan has shallow, set-in sleeves, and buttons to a V-neck. The pattern is wide rib broken with garter stitch and eyelet ridges, and all borders are garter stitch. The yarn is machine-washable, soft cotton D.K.

BACK

With No. 10 (3¼ mm) needles cast on 105 (115) (125) (135) sts and work in gst for 25 rows. **Increase row:** K6 (11) (5) (10), UP1, [K4 (4) (5) (5), up1] to last 7 (12) (5) (10) sts, k to end – 129 (139) (149) (159) sts.
Change to No. 8 (4 mm) needles and work in pattern as follows: **1st row (right side):** All k. **2nd row:** All k. **3rd row:** K4, [yf, k2tog, k3] to end of row. **4th row:** All k. **5th row:** All k. **6th row:** K4, [p1, k4] to end of row. **7th row:** P4, [k1, p4] to end of row. **8th to 18th rows:** Repeat the 6th and 7th rows, 5 times more, then work the 6th row again. The last 18 rows form a repeat of the pattern for the back. Work in pattern for a further 90 rows.
SHAPE ARMHOLES: Keeping continuity of pattern where possible, cast off 3 sts at beginning of each of the next 2 rows, then 2 sts at the beginning of each of the following 2 rows. Dec 1 st at each end of the next row and the 2 following alternate rows – 113 (123) (133) (143) sts. Work in pattern for a further 46 (46) (46) (50) rows.
TO DIVIDE FOR BACK NECK: Next row: Pattern 43 (47) (51) (55) and leave these sts on a spare needle for left back neck and shoulder, pattern 27 (29) (31) (33) and leave these sts on a st holder for back neckband, pattern to end and work on remaining 43 (47) (51) (55) sts for right back neck and shoulder.
RIGHT BACK NECK AND SHOULDER: Pattern 1 row, then cast off 2 sts at the beginning of the next row and the 3 following alternate rows – 35 (39) (43) (47) sts. Work in pattern for 2 rows. Cast off for shoulder.

LEFT BACK NECK AND SHOULDER: With right side of work facing, rejoin yarn to inner end of sts on spare needle and cast off 2 sts at the beginning of the next row and the 3 following alternate rows – 35 (39) (43) (47) sts. Work in pattern for 3 rows. Cast off for shoulder.

LEFT FRONT

With No. 10 (3¼ mm) needles cast on 49 (54) (59) (64) sts and work in gst for 25 rows. **Increase row:** K7 (5) (7) (5), up1, [k4 (5) (5) (6), up1] to last 6 (4) (7) (5) sts, k to end - 59 (64) (69) (74) sts.
Change to No. 8 (4 mm) needles. Work 108 rows in pattern as given for back.
SHAPE ARMHOLE AND NECK: 1st row: Cast off 3 sts, pattern to last 2 sts, dec. **2nd row:** Pattern to end. **3rd row:** Cast off 2 sts, pattern to end. **4th row:** Dec, pattern to end. **5th row:** Dec, pattern to end. **6th row:** Pattern to end. **7th row:** Dec, pattern to last 2 sts, dec.. **8th row:** Pattern to end. **9th row:** Dec, pattern to end – 48 (53) (58) (63) sts. Keeping armhole edge straight, dec 1 st at neck edge on the next row and the 12 (13) (14) (15) following 3rd rows – 35 (39) (43) (47) sts. Work in pattern for a further 20 (17) (14) (15) rows. Cast off for shoulder.

RIGHT FRONT

With No. 10 (3¼ mm) needles cast on 49 (54) (59) (64) sts and work in gst for 25 rows. **Increase row:** K6 (4) (7) (5), up1, [rib 4 (5) (5) (6), up1] to last 7 (5) (7) (5) sts, k to end – 59 (64) (69) (74) sts.
Change to No. 8 (4 mm) needles. Work 108 rows in pattern as given for back.
SHAPE ARMHOLES AND NECK: 1st row: Dec, pattern to end. **2nd row:** Cast off 3 sts, pattern to end. **3rd row:** Pattern to end. **4th row:** Cast off 2 sts, pattern to last 2 sts, dec. **5th row:** Pattern to

last 2 sts, dec. **6th row:** Pattern to end. **7th row:** Dec, pattern to last 2 sts, dec. **8th row:** Pattern to end. **9th row:** Pattern to last 2 sts, dec. – 48 (53) (58) (63) sts. Keeping arm-hole edge straight, dec 1 st at neck edge on the next row and the 12 (13) (14) (15) fol-lowing 3rd rows – 35 (39) (43) (47) sts.Work in pattern for a further 20 (17) (14) (15) rows. Cast off for shoulder.

SLEEVES

With No. 10 (3¼ mm) needles cast on 54 (54) (54) (60) sts and work in gst for 25 rows. **Increase row:** [K5 (5) (5) (4), up1] to last 4 sts, k to end – 64 (64) (64) (74) sts. Change to No. 8 (4 mm) needles and work 4 rows in pattern as given for back. Maintaining continuity of pattern to match back, taking extra sts into pattern as they occur, inc 1 st at each end of the next row and the 24 fol-lowing 4th rows – 114 (114) (114) (124) sts. Work in pattern for a further 3 rows. **SHAPE SLEEVE TOP:** Cast off 3 sts at the begin-ning of each of the next 2 rows, then 2 sts at the beginning of each of the following 2 rows. Dec 1 st at each end of the next row and the 2 following alternate rows – 98 (98) (98) (108) sts. Work 1 row. Cast off.

BUTTONHOLE BORDER

With right side of work facing, using No. 10 (3¼ mm) needles, pick up and k89 sts up row-ends of right front to first front dec, then 52 (52) (52) (56) sts to shoulder – 141 (141) (141) (145) sts. Work in gst for 2 rows. **1st buttonhole row:** K52 (52) (52) (56), cast off 5 sts kwise, [k a further 14, cast off 5 sts kwise] 4 times, k. to end. **2nd buttonhole row:** K to end, casting on 5 sts over each cast off group in previous row. Work in gst for a further 3 rows. Cast off kwise.

BUTTON BORDER

With right side of work facing, using No. 10 (3¼ mm) needles, pick up and k52 (52) (52) (56) sts from shoulder of left front to first front dec, then 89 sts down straight row-ends to cast-on edge – 141 (141) (141) (145) sts. Work in gst for 7 rows. Cast off kwise.

BACK NECKBAND

With right side of work facing, using No. 10 (3¼ mm) needles, pick up and k11 sts down row-ends of right back neck shaping, k across the 27 (29) (31) (33) sts at centre back neck, then pick up and k11 sts up row-ends of left back neck shaping – 49 (51) (53) (55) sts. Work in gst for 7 rows. Cast off kwise.

TO MAKE UP

Do not press. Join shoulder seams, then join row-ends of button and buttonhole borders to row-ends of back neckband. Set sleeves into armholes. Join side and sleeve seams. Add buttons to correspond with buttonholes.

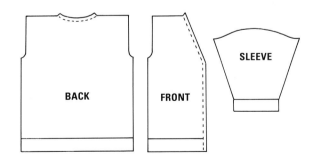

45

SILKY TOUCH

STEP OUT IN THIS STYLISH WAISTCOAT THAT LOOKS
AS GOOD AS IT FEELS

MEASUREMENTS To fit sizes 86 (91) (97) cm/34 (36) (38) in.

Actual measurement 95.5 (101) (106.5) cm/37½ (39¾) (41¾) in. **Side seam** All sizes 37.5 cm/14¾ in.

Length 59.5 (60) (61) cm/23¼ (23½) (24) in.

MATERIALS

10 (11) (12) 50 g balls of Hayfield Next Edition D.K; a pair each of No. 7 (4½ mm) and No. 9 (3¾ mm) knitting needles; a cable needle; 5 buttons. Yarn used: Suede (041).
For stockists, write to Hayfield Textiles Ltd., Glusburn, Keighley, West Yorkshire BD20 8QP.

TENSION

22 stitches and 30 rows to 10 x 10 cm/4 x 4 in, over stocking stitch, and 38-stitch panel to measure 9 cm (3½ in) in width, using No. 7 (4½ mm) needles.

NOTE

Instructions are given for 86 cm/34 in size. Where they vary, work figures in round brackets for larger sizes. Instructions in square brackets are worked as stated after 2nd bracket.

This attractive waistcoat has shaped armholes, pockets, and a V-neck. It is worked in stocking stitch, with woven cable panels in a silky ribbon machine-washable nylon D.K.

BACK

With No. 9 (3¾ mm) needles cast on 111 (117) (123) sts and, beginning odd-numbered rows with k1 and even-numbered rows with p1, work 22 rows in single rib.
Change to No. 7 (4½ mm) needles. Beginning with a k row, ss 90 rows.
FOR ARMHOLES: Cast off 7 (8) (9) sts at beginning of next 2 rows, then dec 1 st each end of next row and the 7 following alternate rows – 81 (85) (89) sts. Ss 49 (51) (53) rows.
FOR SHOULDERS: Cast off 8 sts at beginning of next 4 rows, and 8 (9) (10) sts on following 2 rows. Cast off 33 (35) (37) sts.

POCKET LININGS

With No. 7 (4½ mm) needles cast on 26 sts and ss 29 rows. **Increase row:** [P1, inc] to last 2 sts, p2 - 38 sts. Leave sts on a st holder.

LEFT FRONT

With No. 9 (3¾ mm) needles cast on 61 (63) (67) sts and work 21 rows in rib as on back.
Increase row: Rib 9 and leave these sts on safety-pin for button band, rib 12 (14) (16), [inc, rib 1] 13 (14) (13) times, rib to end – 65 (68) (71) sts. Change to No. 7 (4½ mm) needles. **1st foundation row:** K15 (16) (17), for panel p2, [k3, p2, k6, p2, k3, p2] twice, k12 (14) (16). **2nd foundation row:** P12 (14) (16), for panel k2, [p3, k2, p6, k2, p3, k2] twice, p15 (16) (17).

Work pattern thus: **1st pattern row:** K15 (16) (17), for panel p2, [k3, p2, c6rt, p2, k3, p2] twice, k to end. **2nd and every alternate row:** K and p to end with sts as set. **3rd row:** K to panel, p2, [k3, p2, k6, p2, k3, p2] twice, k to end. **4th row:** As 2nd row. **5th to 8th rows:** As 1st to 4th rows. **9th row:** K to panel, p2, [c8rt, c8lt, p2] twice, k to end. **11th row:** K to panel, p2, [k6, p4, k6, p2] twice, k to end. **13th row:** K to panel, p2, [k3, c5lt, c5rt, k3, p2] twice, k to end. **14th row:** As 2nd row. **15th row:** K to panel, p2, [k3, p2, c6lt, p2, k3, p2] twice, k to end. **16th row:** As 2nd row. **17th to 22nd rows:** As 9th to 14th rows. These 22 rows form the pattern. Work another 6 rows. **Pocket row:** Pattern 15 (16) (17), sl next 38 sts on to st holder and leave at front, and in their place pattern across 38 sts of one pocket lining, pattern to end of row. Pattern 47 rows.
SHAPE FRONT: Keeping continuity of panel, dec 1 st at end of next row and following 6th row – 63 (66) (69) sts. Pattern 5 rows.
FOR ARMHOLE: 1st row: Cast off 7 (8) (9), pattern to last 2 sts, dec. Work 1 row. ** Dec 1 st at armhole edge on next row and 7 following alternate rows, at the same time, dec at front edge on 5th of these rows and following 6th row – 45 (47) (49) sts. Work 1 row, then dec at front edge on next row and 6 (7) (8) following 6th rows – 38 (39) (40) sts. Pattern 11 (7) (3) rows – pattern 12 (8) (4) rows here for right front.
FOR SHOULDER: Cast off 12 sts at beginning of next row and following alternate row. Work 1 row. Cast off 14 (15) (16) sts.

RIGHT FRONT

With No. 9 (3¾ mm) needles cast on 61 (63) (67) sts and work 4 rows in rib as on back.
1st buttonhole row: Rib 3, cast off 3, rib to end. **2nd buttonhole row:** Rib to end, casting on 3 sts over those cast off in previous row. Rib 15 rows. **Increase row:** Rib 15 (16) (17), [inc,

rib 1] 13 (14) (13) times, rib to last 9 sts, turn, leave 9 sts on a safety-pin – 65 (68) (71) sts. Change to No. 7 (4½ mm) needles. **1st foundation row:** K12 (14) (16), for panel p2, [k3, p2, k6, p2, k3, p2] twice, k15 (16) (17). **2nd foundation row:** P15 (16) (17), k2, [p3, k2, p6, k2, p3, k2] twice, p to end. Work pattern thus: **1st pattern row:** K12 (14) (16), for panel p2, [k3, p2, c6rt, p2, k3, p2] twice, k to end. **2nd and every alternate row:** K and p to end with sts as set. **3rd to 22nd rows:** Work as left front. These 22 rows form the pattern. Pattern a further 6 rows. **Pocket row:** Pattern 12 (14) (16), sl next 38 sts on to a st holder and leave at front of work, and in their place, pattern across 38 sts of other pocket lining, pattern to end. Pattern 47 rows. **SHAPE FRONT:** Dec at beginning of next row and 2 following 6th rows – 62 (65) (68) sts. **FOR ARMHOLE:** Cast off 7 (8) (9) sts at beginning of next row. Work as left front from ** to end, noting variation.

POCKET TOPS

With right side facing, rejoin yarn to 38 sts on st holder and using No. 9 (3¾ mm) needles k3, [dec, k3] 7 times – 31 sts. Beginning with an odd-numbered row, work 7 rows in single rib. Cast off in rib.

BUTTONHOLE BAND

Join shoulder seams. With wrong side facing, rejoin yarn to inner end of sts, and using No. 9 (3¾ mm) needles, rib 5 rows. Work the 2 buttonhole rows of right front, then rib 20 rows. Repeat last 22 rows, twice more, then the 2 buttonhole rows again. Continue in rib until band fits up right front and round to centre back neck. Cast off when correct length is assured.

BUTTON BAND

With right side facing, rejoin yarn to inner end of sts on safety-pin, and using No. 9 (3¾ mm) needles, work in rib until band fits up left front, and round to centre back neck, casting off when correct length is assured.

ARMHOLE BORDERS

With right side facing, rejoin yarn and using No. 9 (3¾ mm) needles, pick up and k137 (143) (149) sts evenly round armhole edges. Beginning with an odd-numbered row, work 7 rows in single rib as on back. Cast off in rib.

TO MAKE UP

Do not press. Join side seams, including borders. Sew front bands in place, then join cast-off edges at centre back neck. Sew down pocket linings to wrong side, and row-ends of pocket tops to right side. Add buttons.

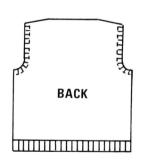
BACK

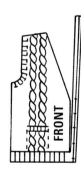
FRONT

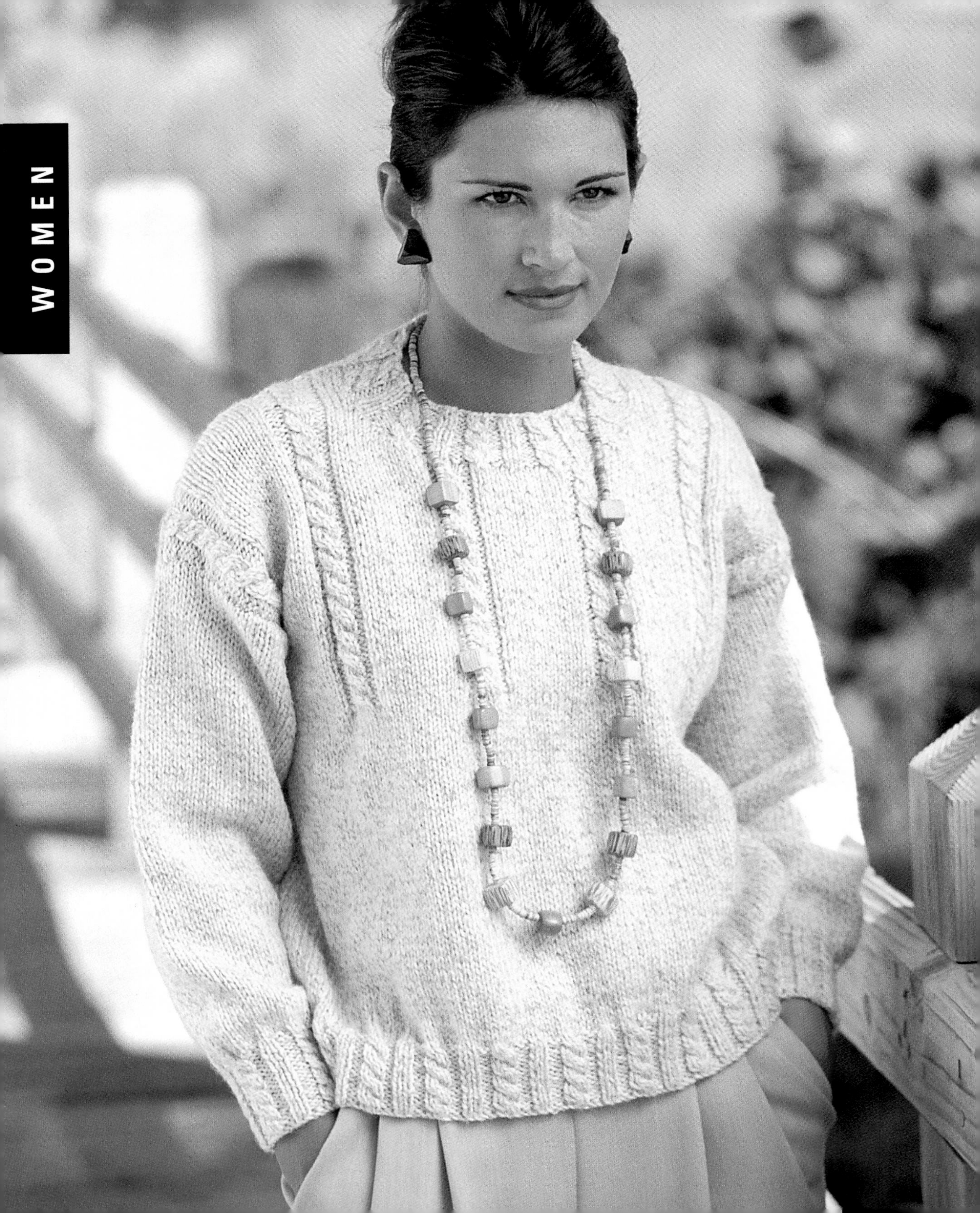

CREAM CABLES

Relax in this simple, easy-to-wear sweater

MEASUREMENTS To fit sizes 81 (86-91) (97-102) cm/32 (36-36) (38-40) in.

Actual measurement 93.5 (104) (114.5) cm/36¾ (41) (45) in. **Side seam** All sizes 30.5 cm/12 in.

Length 55 (56) (56.5) cm/21½ (22) (22¼) in. **Sleeve seam** All sizes 41 cm/16 in.

MATERIALS

5 (5) (6) 100 g balls of Spectrum Strata Aran; No. 6 (5 mm) and No. 8 (4 mm) knitting needles; a cable needle. Yarn used: Peat (258).

For stockists, write to Spectrum Yarns, Spa Mills, New Street, Slaithwaite, Huddersfield, West Yorkshire HD7 5BB.

TENSION

19 stitches and 24 rows, to 10 x 10 cm/4 x 4 in, over the stocking stitch and 26 rows to measure 10 cm/4 in in depth, over the yoke pattern, using No. 6 (5 mm) knitting needles.

NOTE

Instructions are given for 86 cm/34 in size. Where they vary, work figures in round brackets for larger sizes. Work instructions in square brackets as stated after the 2nd bracket.

A classic-style sweater knitted in stocking stitch, with easy-to-knit cable panels on the yoke. The welts and neckband are wide rib and cable. The garment has dropped shoulders and a round neck. The yarn is machine-washable, acrylic/wool Aran weight.

BACK

With No. 8 (4 mm) needles cast on 83 (92) (101) sts and work in cable and rib as follows: **1st (increase) rib row:** K2, [p2, k1, inc, k1, p2, k2] to end - 92 (102) (112) sts. **2nd rib row:** P2, [k2, p4, k2, p2] to end. **3rd rib row:** K2, [p2, c4f, p2, k2] to end. **4th rib row:** As 2nd rib row. **5th rib row:** K2, [p2, k4, p2, k2] to end. The 2nd to 5th rib rows form a repeat of the cable and rib. Repeat 2nd to 5th rib rows, twice more, then the 2nd to 3rd rib rows again. **Next (decrease) row:** P to end, decreasing 3 sts evenly across the row - 89 (99) (109) sts.
Change to No. 6 (5 mm) needles and, beginning with a k row, ss 55 rows. **Next (increase) row:** P7 (9) (9), up1, [p15 (16) (18), up1] to last 7 (10) (10) sts, p to end – 95 (105) (115) sts. Work yoke cable pattern as follows: **1st row:** P3, [k4, p2, k9 (11) (13), p2] to last 7 sts, k4, p3. **2nd row:** K3, p4, [k2, p9 (11) (13), k2, p4] to last 3 sts, k3. **3rd row:** P3, [c4f, p2, k9 (11) (13), p2] to last 7 sts, c4f, p3. **4th row:** As 2nd row.
These 4 rows form a repeat of the yoke pattern. Mark each end of the last row, to denote end of side seams. Pattern a further 54 (56) (58) rows.
FOR SHOULDERS: Cast off 5 (7) (7) sts at the beginning of each of the next 2 rows, 6 (7) (7) sts at the beginning of each of the following 2 rows, then 6 (6) (7) sts at the beginning of each of the next 6 rows. Leave remaining 37 (41) (45) sts on a spare needle.

FRONT

Work as given for back to markers. Pattern a further 33 (35) (37) rows.
DIVIDE STS FOR FRONT NECK: Next row: Pattern 39 (42) (45) and leave these sts on a spare needle for right front neck, pattern the next 17 (21) (25) and leave these sts on a st holder for neckband, pattern to end and work on remaining 39 (42) (45) sts for left front neck.
LEFT FRONT NECK: Dec 1 st at neck edge on each of the next 7 rows and then on the 3 following alternate rows – 29 (32) (35) sts. Pattern a further 7 rows.
FOR SHOULDER: Cast off 5 (7) (7) sts at the beginning of the next row, 6 (7) (7) sts on the following alternate row, then 6 (6) (7) sts on the next 2 alternate rows - 6 (6) (7) sts. Pattern 1 row. Cast off.
RIGHT FRONT NECK: With right side of work facing, rejoin yarn to inner end of sts on spare needle. Dec 1 st at neck edge on each of the next 7 rows and then on the 3 following alternate rows – 29 (32) (35) sts. Pattern another 8 rows.
FOR SHOULDER: Cast off 5 (7) (7) sts at the beginning of the next row, 6 (7) (7) sts on the following alternate row, then 6 (6) (7) sts on the next 2 alternate rows – 6 (6) (7) sts. Pattern 1 row. Cast off.

SLEEVES

With No. 8 (4 mm) needles cast on 38 sts and work in cable and rib as follows: **1st (increase) rib row:** K2, [p2, k1, inc, k1, p2, k2] to end – 42 sts. **2nd rib row:** P2, [k2, p4, k2, p2] to end. **3rd rib row:** K2, [p2, c4f, p2, k2] to end. **4th rib row:** As 2nd rib row. **5th row:** K2, [p2, k4, p2, k2] to end. The 2nd to 5th rows form the cable and rib. Repeat 2nd to 5th rows, 3 times more, then the 2nd and 3rd rows again. **Next (increase) row:** P3 (4) (6), up1, [p5 (3) (2), up1] to last 4 (5) (6) sts, p to end — 50 (54) (58) sts.

Change to No. 6 (5 mm) needles and beginning with a k row, ss 4 rows. Continuing in ss and taking extra sts into ss as they occur, inc 1 st at each end of the next row and the 13 following 5th rows — 78 (82) (86) sts. Beginning with a k row, ss a further 12 rows. Cast off straight across for top of sleeve.

NECKBAND

Join right shoulder seam. With right side of work facing and using No. 8 (4 mm) needles, pick up and k20 sts down left front neck, k across the 17 (21) (25) sts on st holder at centre front, pick up and k20 sts up right front neck, then k across the 37 (41) (45) sts at back neck, decreasing 2 sts (nil) (increasing 2 sts) evenly across these sts — 92 (102) (112) sts. Work in cable and rib as follows:
1st rib row: P2, [k2, p4, k2, p2] to end. **2nd rib row:** K2, [p2, c4f, p2, k2] to end. **3rd row:** As 1st row. **4th rib row:** K2, [p2, k4, p2, k2] to end. Repeat the last 4 rows, once more, then the 1st to 3rd rows again. Cast off loosely in rib, working k1, k2tog, k1 across each 4-st cable as you cast off.

TO MAKE UP

Press as given on ball band. Join left shoulder seam, continuing seam across neckband. Sew cast-off edge of sleeves to row-ends above markers on back and front. Join sleeve and side seams.

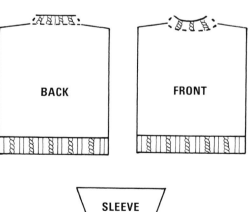

BACK

FRONT

SLEEVE

Out
of the
Blue

———

STYLISH CASUAL WEAR THAT FEATURES TRAVELLING DIAMOND AND ZIG-ZAG PANELS

MEASUREMENTS To fit sizes 97 (102) (107) cm/38 (40) (42) in.

Actual measurement 124.5 (129) (133.5) cm/49 (50¾) (52½) in. **Length** 72 (72) (72.5 cm/28¼ (28¼) (28½) in.

Side seam All sizes 45.5 cm/17¾ in. **Sleeve seam** All sizes 46 cm/18 in.

MATERIALS

8 (9) (10) 100 g balls of Littlewoods Soft Cotton Aran; No. 7 (4½ mm) and No. 9 (3¾ mm) knitting needles; a No. 9 (3¾ mm) circular knitting needle; a cable needle; 5 buttons. Yarn used: Denim.
For stockists, write to Andrea Wood, Littlewoods Chainstore Ltd, Atlantic Pavilion, Albert Dock, Liverpool L70 7AD.

TENSION

16 stitches and 23 rows, to measure 9 x 9 cm/3½ x 3½ in, over reverse stocking stitch, a 27-stitch diamond panel to measure 12 cm/4¾ in, and 20-stitch zig-zag panel to measure 9.5 cm/3¾ in, using No. 7 (4½ mm) needles.

NOTE

Instructions are given for 97 cm/38 in size. Work figures in round brackets for larger sizes. Work instructions in square brackets as stated after 2nd bracket.

This cardigan has dropped shoulders and buttons to a V-neck. It's knitted in reverse stocking stitch, with travelling diamond and zig-zag panels.

BACK

With No. 9 (3¾ mm) needles cast on 101 (105) (109) sts. Beginning odd-numbered rows with k1 and even-numbered rows with p1, rib 19 rows. **Increase row:** Rib nil (2) (4), inc, [rib 3, inc] to last nil (2) (4) sts, rib nil (2) (4) - 127 (131) (135) sts. Change to No. 7 (4½ mm) needles. Work 36-row pattern thus: **1st row (right side):** * P4 (6) (8), tw3l, for dmst [p1, k1] 3 times, tw3l, p10, tw3l, p1, tw3l, tw3r, p1, tw3r, p2, tw3r *, p37, ** tw3l, p2, tw3l, p1, tw3l, tw3r, p1, tw3r, p10, tw3r, for dmst [k1, p1] 3 times, tw3r, p4 (6) (8) **. **2nd and alternate rows:** K and p to end with sts as set. **3rd row:** * P5 (7) (9), tw3l, for dmst [p1, k1] 3 times, tw3l, p10, tw3l, p1, k4, p1, tw3r, p2, tw3r *, p39, ** tw3l, p2, tw3l, p1, k4, p1, tw3r, p10, tw3r, for dmst [k1, p1] 3 times, tw3r, p5 (7) (9) **. **4th row:** As 2nd row. These 4 rows form dmst. **5th row:** * P6 (8) (10), tw3l, dmst 6, tw3l, p10, tw3l, p1, k2, p1, tw3r, p2, tw3r, p2, k2 *, p33, ** k2, p2, tw3l, p2, tw3l, p1, k2, p1, tw3r, p10, tw3r, dmst 6, tw3r, p to end **. **7th row:** * P7 (9) (11), tw3l, dmst 6, tw3l, p10, tw3l, p2, tw3r, p2, tw3r, p2, k4 *, p31, ** k4, p2, tw3l, p2, tw3l, p2, tw3r, p10, tw3r, dmst 6, tw3r, p to end **. **9th row:** * P8 (10) (12), tw3l, dmst 6, tw3l, p10, tw3l, tw3r, p2, tw3r, p2, tw3r, tw3l *, p29, ** tw3r, tw3l, p2, tw3l, p2, tw3l, tw3r, p10, tw3r, dmst 6, tw3r, p to end **. **11th row:** * P9 (11) (13), tw3l, dmst 6, tw3l, p10, k4, p2, tw3r, p2, tw3r, p2, tw3l *, p27, ** tw3r, p2, tw3l, p2, tw3l, p2, k4, p10, tw3r, dmst 6, tw3r, p to end **. **13th row:** * P10 (12) (14), tw3l, dmst 6, tw3l, p10, k2, p2, tw3r, p2, tw3r, p1, k2, p1, tw3l *, p25, ** tw3r, p1, k2, p1, tw3l, p2, tw3l, p2, k2, p10, tw3r, dmst 6, tw3r, p to end **.

15th row: * P11 (13) (15), tw3l, dmst 6, tw3l, p12, tw3r, p2, tw3r, p1, k4, p1, tw3l *, p23, ** tw3r, p1, k4, p1, tw3l, p2, tw3l, p12, tw3l, dmst 6, tw3r, p to end **. **17th row:** * P12 (14) (16), tw3l, dmst 6, tw3l, p10, tw3r, p2, tw3r, p1, tw3r, tw3l, p1, tw3l *, p21, ** tw3r, p1, tw3r, tw3l, p1, tw3l, p2, tw3l, p10, tw3r, dmst 6, tw3r, p to end **. **19th row:** * P12 (14) (16), tw3r, dmst 6, tw3r, p10, tw3l, p2, tw3l, p1, tw3l, tw3r, p1, tw3r *, p21, ** tw3l, p1, tw3l, tw3r, p1, tw3r, p1, tw3r, p2, tw3r, p10, tw3l, dmst 6, tw3l, p to end **. **21st row:** * P11 (13) (15), tw3r, dmst 6, tw3r, p12, tw3l, p2, tw3l, p1, k4, p1, tw3r *, p23, ** tw3l, p1, k4, p1, tw3r, p2, tw3r, p12, tw3l, dmst 6, tw3l, p to end **. **23rd row:** * P10 (12) (14), tw3r, dmst 6, tw3r, p10, k2, p2, tw3l, p2, tw3l, p1, k2, p1, tw3r *, p25, ** tw3l, p1, k2, p1, tw3r, p2, tw3r, p2, k2, p10, tw3l, dmst 6, tw3l, p to end **. **25th row:** * P9 (11) (13), tw3r, dmst 6, tw3r, p10, k4, p2, tw3l, p2, tw3l, p2, tw3r *, p27, ** tw3l, p2, tw3r, p2, tw3r, p2, k4, p10, tw3l, dmst 6, tw3l, p to end **. **27th row:** * P8 (10) (12), tw3r, dmst 6, tw3r, p10, tw3r, tw3l, p2, tw3l, p2, tw3l, tw3r *, p29, ** tw3l, tw3r, p2, tw3r, p2, tw3r, tw3l, p10, tw3l, dmst 6, tw3l, p to end **. **29th row:** * P7 (9) (11), tw3r, dmst 6, tw3r, p10, tw3r, tw3l, p2, tw3l, p2, k4 *, p31, ** k4, p2, tw3r, p2, tw3r, p2, tw3l, p10, tw3l, dmst 6, tw3l, p to end **. **31st row:** * P6 (8) (10), tw3r, dmst 6, tw3r, p10, tw3r, p1, k2, p1, tw3l, p2, tw3l, p2, k2 *, p33, ** k2, p2, tw3r, p2, tw3r, p1, k2, p1, tw3l, p10, tw3l, dmst 6, tw3l, p to end **. **33rd row:** * P5 (7) (9), tw3r, dmst 6, tw3r, p10, tw3r, p1, k4, p1, tw3l, p2, tw3l *, p39, ** tw3r, p2, tw3r, p1, k4, p1, tw3l, p10, tw3l, dmst 6, tw3l, p to end **. **35th row:** * P4 (6) (8), tw3r, dmst 6, tw3r, p10, tw3r, p1, tw3r, tw3l, p1, tw3l, p2, tw3l *, p37, ** tw3r, p2, tw3r, p1, tw3r, tw3l, p1, tw3l, p10, tw3l, dmst 6, tw3l, p to end **. **36th row:** As 2nd row. Pat-tern another 62 rows. Mark each end of last row for side seams. Pattern

64 (64) (66) rows.

FOR SHOULDERS: Cast off 23 (23) (24) sts at beginning of next 2 rows and 23 (24) (24) sts on following 2 rows. Leave 35 (37) (39) sts on a holder.

FRONT

LEFT FRONT: With No. 9 (3¾ mm) needles cast on 49 (51) (53) sts. Rib 19 rows as on back. **Increase row:** Rib 2 (3) (4), inc, [rib 3, inc] to last 2 (3) (4) sts, rib to end – 61 (63) (65) sts. Change to No. 7 (4½ mm) needles. Place pattern thus: *** **1st row:** Work from * to * on 1st row of back, p to end. **2nd and alternate rows:** K and p to end with sts as set. **3rd row:** Work from * to * on 3rd row of back, p to end. **** These 3 rows place pattern. Keeping pattern correct as set, work another 89 rows.
SHAPE FRONT: Dec 1 st at front edge on next row and 14 (15) (16) following 4th rows – 46 (47) (48) sts. Mark side edge of 6th row. Pattern 13 (9) (7) rows – pattern 14 (10) (8) rows for right front.
FOR SHOULDER: Cast off 23 (23) (24) sts at beginning of next row – 23 (24) (24) sts. Work 1 row. Cast off.
RIGHT FRONT: Work as left front to ***. **1st row:** P16, work from ** to ** on 1st row of back. **2nd and alternate rows:** K and p to end with sts as set. **3rd row:** P17, work from ** to ** on 3rd row of back. Work as left front from ****, noting variation.

SLEEVES

LEFT SLEEVE: With No. 9 (3¾ mm) needles cast on 43 (43) (47) sts. Rib 19 rows as on back. **Increase row:** Rib 5 (5) (7), inc, [rib 1, inc] to last 5 (5) (7) sts, rib to end – 60 (60) (64) sts. Change to No. 7 (4½ mm) needles. Work pattern thus: ***** **1st row (right side):** P20 (20) (22), tw3l, [p1, k1] 3 times, tw3l, p to end. **2nd and every alternate row:** K and p to end with sts as set. **3rd increase row:** Inc,

p20 (20) (22), tw3l, [p1, k1] 3 times, tw3l, p to last st, inc – 62 (62) (66) sts. ****** Keeping zig-zag panel correct as back, working extra sts in rss as they occur, work 4 rows, then inc 1 st each end of next row and 15 (15) (14) following 5th rows – 94 (94) (96) sts. Pattern 17 (17) (22) rows. Cast off.
RIGHT SLEEVE: Work as left sleeve to *****.
1st row (right side): P28 (28) (30), tw3r, [k1, p1] 3 times, tw3r, p to end. **2nd and alternate rows:** K and p to end with sts as set. **3rd increase row:** Inc, p26 (26) (28), tw3r, [k1, p1] 3 times, tw3r, p to last st, inc – 62 (62) (66) sts. Work as left sleeve from ****** to end.

FRONT BORDER

Join shoulder seams. With right side facing, using No. 9 (3¾ mm) circular needle, pick up and k90 sts up right front to 1st front dec, 73 (73) (75) sts to shoulder, k35 (37) (39) sts across back neck, pick up and k73 (73) (75) sts down left front to 1st front dec, then 90 sts down to lower edge – 361 (363) (369) sts. Working backwards and forwards in rows, k1 row and p2 rows. Rib 3 rows as on back. **Buttonhole row:** Rib 4, k2tog, yrn, [rib 19, k2tog, yf or yrn] 4 times, rib to end. Rib 4 rows. Cast off in rib.

TO MAKE UP

Press as on ball band. Sew cast-off edge of sleeves above markers on back and fronts. Join side and sleeve seams. Add buttons.

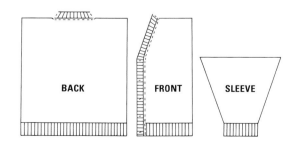

BACK   FRONT   SLEEVE

FISHING PARTNERS

THEY'RE AN EYE-CATCHING PAIR IN MATCHING ARAN-STYLE FISHERMAN'S SWEATERS

MEASUREMENTS To fit sizes 66 (71-76) (81-86) (91) (97-102) (107-112) (117-127) cm/26 (28-30) (32-34) (36) (38-40) (42-44) (46-48) in.

Actual measurement 76.5 (86) (95) (104.5) (123.5) (133) (142.5) cm/30¼ (34) (37½) (41) (48½) (52¼) (56¼) in.

Side seam 23 (25) (27) (29) (40.5) (40.5) (40.5) cm/9 (10) (10¾) (11½) (16) (16) (16) in.

Length 39 (42.5) (45.5) (49) (68.5) (69.5) (70) cm/15¼ (16¾) (18) (19¼) (27) (27¼) (27½) in.

Sleeve seam 28.5 (30.5) (32.5) (34.5) (49.5) (49.5) (49.5) cm/11¼ (12) (12¾) (13½) (19½) (19½) (19½) in.

MATERIALS

4 (4) (5) (6) (8) (9) (10) 100 g balls of Spectrum Braeside Aran; No. 7 (4½ mm) and No. 9 (3¾ mm) knitting needles. Yarn used: Saxe and Cream.
For stockists, write to Spectrum Yarns Ltd, Spa Mills, New Street, Slaithwaite, Huddersfield HD7 5BB.

TENSION

17 stitches and 30 rows, to 10 x 10 cm/4 x 4 in, over the pattern, using No. 7 (4½mm) needles.

NOTE

Instructions are given for 66 cm/26 in size. Where they vary, work figures in round brackets for larger sizes. Work instructions in square brackets as stated after the 2nd bracket.

These sweaters have dropped shoulders and a round neck. The pattern is textured bands formed by easy knit and purl stitches, and separated by garter-stitch ridges. The borders are double rib. The yarn is machine-washable acrylic/wool Aran.

BACK

With No. 9 (3¾ mm) needles cast on 62 (70) (78) (86) (102) (110) (118) sts and, beginning odd-numbered rows with k2 and even-numbered rows with p2, work 13 (13) (13) (13) (19) 19) (19) rows in double rib.
Increase row: Rib 16 (18) (20) (22) (26) (28) (30), up1, [Rib 15 (17) (19) (21) (25) (27) (29), up1] twice, rib 16 (18) (20) (22) (26) (28) (30) - 65 (73) (81) (89) (105) (113) (121) sts.
Change to No. 7 (4½mm) needles.
1st to 5th rows: All k. 6th row: All p. **7th row:** K4, [p1, k7] to last 5 sts, p1, k4. **8th row:** P3, [k1, p1, k1, p5] to last 6 sts, k1, p1, k1, p3. **9th row:** K2, [p1, k3] to last 3 sts, p1, k2. **10th row:** P1, [k1, p5, k1, p1] to last 8 sts, k1, p5, k1, p1. **11th row:** [P1, k3] to last st, p1. **12th row:** P3, [k1, p1, k1, p5] to last 6 sts, k1, p1, k1, p3. **13th to 23rd rows:** As 11th row back to 1st row, in that reverse order. **24th row:** All p. **25th row:** [P1, k3] to last st, p1. **26th row:** P1, [k1, p3] to end. **27th row:** K2, [p1, k3] to last 3 sts, p1, k2. **28th row:** P3, [k1, p3] to last 2 sts, k1, p1. **29th to 35th rows:** As 25th to 28th rows, then the 25th to 27th rows again. **36th row:** All p. **37th to 41st rows:** All k. **42nd row:** All p. **43rd row:** K4, [p1, k7] to last 5 sts, p1, k4. 44th row: P3, [k1, p1, k1, p5] to last 6 sts, k1, p1, k1, p3. **45th row:** K2, [p1, k3] to last 3 sts, p1, k2. **46th row:** P1, k1,[p5, k1, p1, k1] to last 7 sts, p5, k1, p1. **47th row:** P1, [k7, p1] to end. **48th row:** All p. **49th to 53rd rows:** As 43rd to 47th rows. **54th row:** All p. Mark each end of this row for end of side seam for the 1st size. **55th to 59th rows:** All k. **60th row:** All p. Mark each end of this row for end of side seam for the 2nd size. **61st row:** [P1, k3] to last st, p1. **62nd row:** P1, [k1, p3] to end. **63rd row:** K2, [p1, k3] to last 3 sts, p1, k2. **64th row:** [P3, k1] to last st, p1. **65th row:** As 61st row. **66th row:** All k. Mark each end of the last row for end of side seam for the 3rd size. **67th row:** As 61st row. **68th to 71st rows:** As 64th row back to 61st row, in that reverse order. **72nd row:** All p. Mark each end of this row for end of side seams for the 4th size.
These 72 rows form a repeat of the pattern. Pattern another nil (nil) (nil) (nil) (26) (26) (26) rows. Mark each end of the last row for end of side seams for the 5th, 6th and 7th sizes. ** Pattern another 23 (33) (43) (53) (77) (79) (81) rows.
DIVIDE STS FOR BACK NECK: Next row: Pattern 26 (29) (32) (35) (40) (43) (46) and leave these sts on a spare needle for left back neck, pattern the next 13 (15) (17) (19) (25) (27) (29) and leave them on a st holder, pattern to end and work on remaining 26 (29) (32) (35) (40) (43) (46) sts for right back neck.
RIGHT BACK NECK: Dec 1 st at neck edge on each of the next 4 rows – 22 (25) (28) (31) (36) (39) (42) sts. Pattern 2 rows – pattern 3 rows here for left back neck. Cast off for shoulder.
LEFT BACK NECK: With right side facing, rejoin yarn to inner end of sts on spare needle and work as for right back neck, noting variation.

FRONT

Work as given for back to **. Pattern another 13 (23) (33) (41) (61) (63) (65) rows.
DIVIDE STS FOR FRONT NECK: Next row: Pattern 26 (30) (33) (37) (42) (46) (49) and leave these sts on a spare needle for right front neck, pattern the next 13 (13) (15) (15) (21) (21) (23) sts and leave them on a st holder, pat-

60

tern to end and work on remaining 26 (30) (33) (37) (42) (46) (49) sts for left front neck.

LEFT FRONT NECK: Dec 1 st at neck edge on the next 4 (5) (5) (6) (6) (7) (7) rows − 22 (25) (28) (31) (36) (39) (42) sts. Pattern another 12 (11) (11) (12) (16) (15) (15) rows − pattern 13 (12) (12) (13) (17) (16) (16) rows here for right front neck. Cast off for shoulder.

RIGHT FRONT NECK: With right side facing, rejoin yarn to inner end of sts on spare needle and work as for left front neck, noting variation.

SLEEVES

With No. 9 (3¾ mm) needles cast on 30 (34) (38) (42) (46) (50) (54) sts and work 13 (13) (13) (13) (15) (15) (15) rows in rib as given for back.

INCREASE ROW: Rib 8 (5) (10) (6) (12) (7) (14), up1, [rib 7 (4) (9) (5) (11) (6) (13), up1] to last 8 (5) (10) (6) (12) (7) (14) sts, rib to end − 33 (41) (41) (49) (49) (57) (57) sts.

Change to No. 7 (4½ mm) needles and work 6 rows in pattern as given for back. Keeping continuity of pattern to match back, taking extra sts into the pattern as they occur, inc 1 st at each end of the next row and the 10 (8) (11) (9) (22) (19) (20) following 6th (8th) (6th) (8th) (5th) (6th) (6th) rows − 55 (59) (65) (69) (95) (97) (99) sts.
Pattern another 3 (5) (9) (9) (13) (9) (3) rows. Cast off.

NECKBAND

Join right shoulder seam. With right side of work facing and using No. 9 (3¾ mm) needles, pick up and k15 (15) (15) (17) (21) (21) (21) sts down left front neck, k the 13 (13) (15) (15) (21) (21) (21) sts at centre front, pick up and k15 (15) (15) (17) (21) (21) (21) sts up right front neck, 4 sts down right back neck, k the 13 (15) (17) (19) (25) (27) (29) sts at back neck, decreasing 2 (nil) (nil) (2) (2) (nil) (increasing 2 sts) across these sts, pick up and k 4 sts up left back neck − 62 (66) (70) (74) (94) (98) (102) sts. Work 13 (13) (13) (13) (19) (19) (19) rows in rib as given for back. Cast off in rib.

TO MAKE UP

Press as given on ball band. Join left shoulder seam, including neckband. Sew cast-off edge of sleeves above markers on back and front. Join sleeve and side seams. Fold neckband in half to wrong side and slip st in place on the inside.

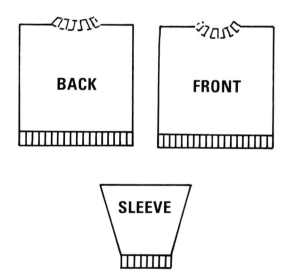

CLASSIC CARDIGAN

THIS ELEGANT CARDIGAN WILL SEE HIM THROUGH ANY OCCASION

MEASUREMENTS To fit sizes 91 (97-102) (107-112) cm/36 (38-40) (42-44) in.

Actual measurement 103 (113) (123.5) cm/40½ (44½) (48½) in. **Side seam** All sizes 48 cm/18¾ in.

Length 77.5 (78.5) (79.5) cm/30½ (31) (31¼) in. **Sleeve seam** All sizes 47.5 cm/18¾ in.

MATERIALS

9 (9) (10) 100 g balls of Littlewoods Soft Aran; No. 7 (4½ mm) and No. 9 (3¾ mm) knitting needles; a cable needle; 5 buttons. Yarn used: Cream.
For stockists, write to Andrea Wood, Littlewoods Chainstore Ltd, Atlantic Pavilion, Albert Dock, Liverpool L70 7AD.

TENSION

18 stitches and 25 rows, to 10 x 10 cm/4 x 4 in, over stocking stitch, 1 cable panel of 17 stitches, to measure 6.5 cm/2½ in in width and 1 ribbed panel of 11 stitches, to measure 4 cm/1½ in in width, using No. 7 (4½ mm) needles.

NOTE

Instructions are given for 91 cm/36 in size. Where they vary, work figures in round brackets for larger sizes. Work instructions in square brackets as stated after 2nd bracket.

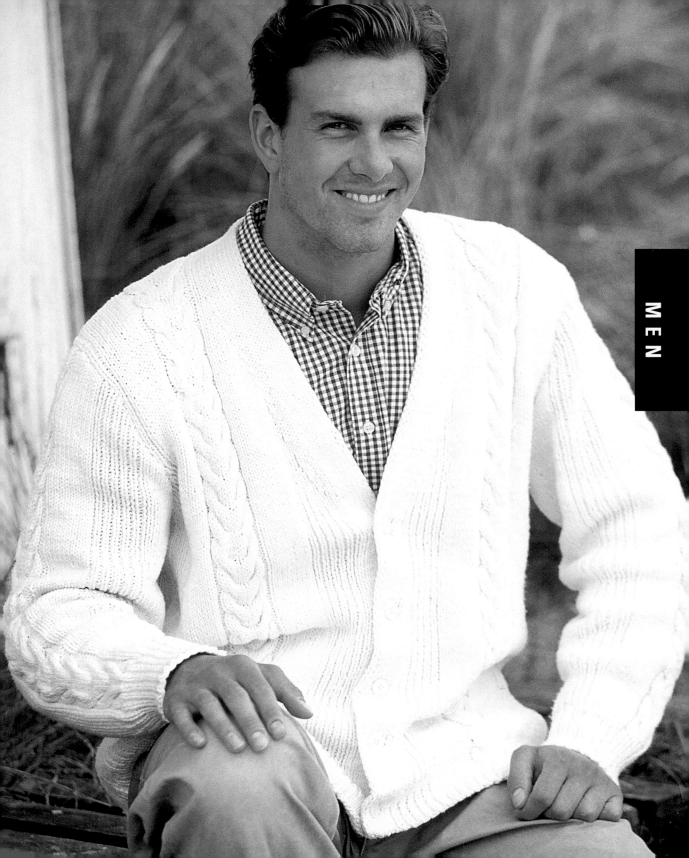

This pattern has cable and rib panels, ribbed cuffs and lower border. The stocking stitch front bands are folded double and knitted with the fronts.

BACK

With No. 9 (3¾ mm) needles cast on 117 (127) (137) sts and, beginning odd-numbered rows with k1 and even-numbered rows with p1, single rib 6 rows. Change to No. 7 (4½ mm) needles. **1st row:** For ss panel k7, * for rib panel p1, [k1, p1] 5 times, for ss panel k5 (7) (9), for cable panel p2, k13, p2, for ss panel k5 (7) (9), for rib panel p1, [k1, p1] 5 times *, for ss panel k5 (7) (9), work from * to * once, for ss panel k7. **2nd and every alternate row:** K and p to end with sts as set. **3rd to 6th rows:** Repeat 1st and 2nd rows, twice more. **7th row:** For ss panel k7, * for rib panel p1, [k1, p1] 5 times, for ss panel k5 (7) (9), for cable panel p2, c6b, k1, c6f, p2, for ss panel k5 (7) (9), for rib panel p1, [k1, p1] 5 times *, for ss panel k5 (7) (9), work from * to * once, for ss panel k7. **8th row:** As 2nd row. These 8 rows form pattern. Pattern another 106 rows.
FOR ARMHOLES: Cast off 5 sts at beginning of next 2 rows, then dec 1 st at each end of next row and 5 (7) (9) following alternate rows – 95 (101) (107) sts. Pattern another 55 (53) (51) rows.
FOR SHOULDERS: Cast off 10 sts at beginning of next 2 rows, then 9 (10) (11) sts at beginning of following 4 rows. Cast off remaining 39 (41) (43) sts.

LEFT FRONT

With No. 9 (3¾ mm) needles cast on 71 (75) (81) sts. **1st row:** [K1, p1] to last 15 (15) (17) sts, k15 (15) (17) for front border. **2nd row:** P7 (7) (8), sl1, p7 (7) (8) for front border, then rib to end. Repeat last 2 rows, twice

more. Change to No. 7 (4½ mm) needles. Place pattern thus: **1st (buttonhole) row:** For ss panel k7, for rib panel p1, [k1, p1] 5 times, for ss panel k5 (7) (9), for cable panel p2, k13, p2, for ss panel k5 (7) (9), for rib panel p1, [k1, p1] 5 times, k2, cast off 3, k a further 4 (4) (6), cast off 3, k1 more. **2nd (buttonhole) row:** P2, turn, cast on 3, turn, p2 (2) (3), sl1, p2 (2) (3), turn, cast on 3, turn, p2, k and p to end with sts as set. Pattern another 112 rows to match back, making double buttonholes as before on 25th and 26th, 51st and 52nd, 77th and 78th and 103rd and 104th of these rows.
SHAPE ARMHOLES AND FRONT EDGE: 1st row: Cast off 5 sts, pattern to last 17 (17) (19) sts, dec, k15 (15) (17). **2nd row:** Pattern to end. **3rd row:** Dec, pattern to last 17 (17) (19) sts, dec, k to end. Repeat 2nd and 3rd rows, 3 times more – 57 (61) (67) sts. **Next row:** Pattern to end. **Next row:** Dec, pattern to end. **Next row:** Pattern to end. **Next row:** As 3rd row – 54 (58) (64) sts.
FOR 2ND SIZE ONLY: 1st row: Pattern to end. **2nd row:** Dec, pattern to end. **3rd row:** As 1st row. **4th row:** Dec, pattern to last 17 sts, dec, k to end – 55 sts.
FOR 3RD SIZE ONLY: 1st row: Pattern to end. **2nd row:** Dec, pattern to end. **3rd row:** As 1st row. **4th row:** Dec, pattern to last 19 sts, dec, k to end. Repeat last 4 rows, once more – 58 sts.
FOR ALL SIZES: Pattern 3 rows, dec 1 st at front edge only on the next row and 9 (8) (7) following 4th rows – 44 (46) (50) sts. Pattern 15 (17) (19) rows.
FOR SHOULDER: Cast off 10 sts at beginning of next row, then 9 (10) (11) sts on 2 following alternate rows – 16 (16) (18) sts. Pattern 19 (21) (23) rows. Cast off.

RIGHT FRONT

With No. 9 (3¾ mm) needles cast on 71 (75) (81) sts. **1st row:** K15 (15) (17), [p1, k1] to end. **2nd row:** Rib to last 15 (15) (17) sts, p7

(7) (8), sl1, p7 (7) (8). Repeat last 2 rows, twice more. Change to No. 7 (4½ mm) needles. **1st row:** K15 (15) (17), for rib panel p1, [k1, p1] 5 times, for ss panel k5 (7) (9), for cable panel p2, k13, p2, for ss panel k5 (7) (9), for rib panel p1, [k1, p1] 5 times, for ss panel k7. 2nd row: K and p as set to last 15 (15) (17) sts, p7 (7) (8), sl1, p7 (7) (8). These 2 rows place pattern. Pattern another 113 rows to match back.

SHAPE ARMHOLE AND FRONT EDGE: 1st row: Cast off 5 sts, pattern to end. **2nd row:** K15 (15) (17), skpo, pattern to last 2 sts, dec. **3rd row:** Pattern to end. Repeat 2nd and 3rd rows, 4 times more. **Next row:** Pattern to last 2 sts, dec. **Next row:** Pattern to end. **Next row:** Pattern 15 (15) (17), skpo, pattern to last nil (2) (2) sts, nil (dec) (dec) − 54 (57) (63) sts.

FOR 2ND SIZE ONLY: 1st row: Pattern to end. **2nd row:** Pattern to last 2 sts, dec. **3rd row:** As 1st row. **4th row:** K15, skpo, pattern to end − 55 sts.

FOR 3RD SIZE ONLY: 1st row: Pattern to end. **2nd row:** Pattern to last 2 sts, dec. **3rd row:** As 1st row. **4th row:** K17, skpo, pattern to last 2 sts, dec. **5th row:** As 1st row. **6th row:** As 2nd row. 7th row: As 1st row. 8th row: K17, skpo, pattern to end − 58 sts.

FOR ALL SIZES: Pattern 3 rows, dec 1 st at front edge only on next row and 9 (8) (7) following 4th rows − 44 (46) (50) sts. Pattern 14 (16) (18) rows.

FOR SHOULDER: Work as for left front − 16 (16) (18) sts. Pattern 18 (20) (22) rows. Cast off.

SLEEVES

With No. 9 (3¾ mm) needles cast on 43 (47) (51) sts, single rib 21 rows as back. **Increase row:** Rib 1 (1) (nil), [rib 2, up1, rib 3, up1] to last 2 (1) (1) st(s), rib to end − 59 (65) (71) sts. Change to No. 7 (4½ mm) needles. **1st row:** For ss panel k5 (6) (7), for rib panel p1, [k1, p1] 5 times, for ss panel k5 (7) (9), for cable panel p2, k13, p2, for ss panel k5

(7) (9), for rib panel p1, [k1, p1] 5 times, for ss panel k5 (6) (7). 2nd row: K and p to end with sts as set. These 2 rows place pattern. Keeping pattern correct to match back, working extra sts in ss as they occur, work 4 rows, then inc 1 st each end of next row and 10 following 8th rows − 81 (87) (93) sts. Pattern 17 rows.

FOR SLEEVE TOP: Cast off 5 sts at beginning of next 2 rows, dec 1 st at each end of next row and 11 (13) (15) following alternate rows − 47 (49) (51) sts. Pattern 1 row, then cast off 3 sts at beginning of next 8 rows. Cast off remaining 23 (25) (27) sts.

TO MAKE UP

Press as given on ball band. Join shoulder seams. Set in sleeves. Join sleeve and side seams. Join cast-off edges of front borders tog, sew to back neck. Fold border in half at sl st and sew down on wrong side. Neaten double buttonholes. Add buttons.

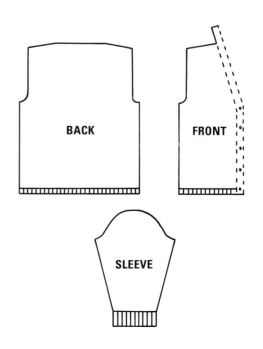

BACK

FRONT

SLEEVE

MEN

PERFECT
MIX

Take time out together in relaxing style

MEASUREMENTS To fit sizes 86 (91) (97) (102) (107) cm/34 (36) (38) (40) (42) in.

Actual measurement 97 (102.5) (106.5) (112) (115.5) cm/38 (40¼) (41¾) (44) (45½) in.

Side seam All sizes 48.5 cm/19 in. **Length** 71 (71) (72.5) (72.5) (73.5) cm/27¾ (27¾) (28½) (28½) (29) in.

Sleeve seam 45.5 (45.5) (45.5) (48.5) (48.5) cm/17¾ (17¾) (17¾) (19) (19) in.

MATERIALS

11 (12) (13) (14) (15) 50 g balls of Pingouin Corrida 4 D.K. in main and 1 ball contrast. No. 8 (4 mm) and No. 10 (3¼ mm) knitting needles; a cable needle; 3 buttons. Yarn used: Marine (518) and Ecru (512).
Key: main = m, contrast = c.
For stockists, write to Habico Ltd, 2 Peary Street, Rochdale Road, Manchester M4 4JB enclosing an SAE.

TENSION

22 stitches and 30 rows, to measure 10 x 10 cm/4 x 4 in, over the pattern, using No. 8 (4 mm) needles.

NOTE

Instructions are given for the 86 cm/34 in size. Where they vary, work figures in round brackets for larger sizes. Work instructions in square brackets as stated after 2nd bracket..

These tops have set-in sleeves and shirt neck-line. Knitted mainly in reverse stocking stitch, the bold panels are worked in easy twist and garter-stitch diamonds.

BACK

With No. 10 (3¼ mm) needles and c cast on 93 (99) (103) (109) (113) sts and, beginning odd-numbered rows with k1, and even-numbered rows with p1, work 2 rows in single rib. Join in m and rib 2 rows m, 2 rows c and rib 19 rows m. Continue with m only.
Increase row: Rib 7 (3) (5) (2) (4), inc., [rib 5 (6) (6) (7) (7), inc] to last 7 (4) (6) (2) (4) sts., rib to end – 107 (113) (117) (123) (127) sts.
Change to No. 8 (4 mm) needles. Work 30-row pattern thus: **1st row (right side):** P14 (14) (16) (16) (18), k4, [p21 (23) (23) (25) (25), k4] 3 times, p to end. **2nd row:** K. and p to end, with sts. as set. **3rd row:** P14 (14) (16) (16) (18), c4b., [p21 (23) (23) (25) (25), c4b] 3 times, p. to end. **4th row:** As 2nd row. **5th row:** P13 (13) (15) (15) (17), cr3 rt., cr3lt, [p19 (21) (21) (23) (23), cr3rt, cr3lt] 3 times, p to end. **6th row:** K13 (13) (15) (15) (17), p2, k2, p2, [k19 (21) (21) (23) (23), p2, k2, p2] 3 times, k to end. **7th row:** P12 (12) (14) (14) (16), cr3rt, k2, cr3lt, [p17 (19) (19) (21) (21), cr3rt, k2, cr3lt] 3 times, p to end. **8th row:** K12 (12) (14) (14) (16), p2, k4, p2, [k17 (19) (19) (21) (21), p2, k4, p2] 3 times, k to end. **9th row:** P11 (11) (13) (13) (15), tw3rt, k4, tw3lt, [p15 (17) (17) (19) (19), tw3rt, k4, tw3lt] 3 times, p to end. **10th row:** K11 (11) (13) (13) (15), p2, k6, p2, [k15 (17) (17) (19) (19), p2, k6, p2] 3 times, k to end. **11th row:** P10 (10) (12) (12) (14), tw3rt, k6, tw3lt, [p13 (15) (15) (17) (17), tw3rt, k6, tw3lt] 3 times, p to end. **12th row:** K10 (10) (12) (12) (14), p2, k8, p2, [k13 (15) (15) (17) (17), p2, k8, p2] 3 times, k to end. **13th row:** P9 (9) (11) (11) (13), tw3r., k8, tw3lt, [p11 (13) (13) (15)

(15), tw3rt, k8, tw3lt] 3 times, p to end. **14th row:** K9 (9) (11) (11) (13), p2, k10, p2, [k11 (13) (13) (15) (15), p2, k10, p2] 3 times, k to end. **15th row:** P8 (8) (10) (10) (12), tw3rt, k10, tw3lt, [p9 (11) (11) (13) (13), tw3rt, k10, tw3lt] 3 times, p to end. **16th row:** K8 (8) (10) (10) (12), p2, k12, p2, [k9 (11) (11) (13) (13), p2, k12, p2] 3 times, k to end. **17th row:** P8 (8) (10) (10) (12), tw3lt, k10, tw3rt, [p9 (11) (11) (13) (13), tw3lt, k10, tw3rt] 3 times, p to end. **18th row:** As 14th row. **19th row:** P9 (9) (11) (11) (13), tw3lt, k8, tw3rt, [p11 (13) (13) (15) (15), tw3lt, k8, tw3rt] 3 times, p to end. **20th row:** As 12th row. **21st row:** P10 (10) (12) (12) (14), tw3lt, k6, tw3rt, [p13 (15) 15) (17) (17), tw3lt, k6, tw3rt] 3 times, p to end. **22nd row:** As 10th row. **23rd row:** P11 (11) (13) (13) (15), tw3lt, k4, tw3rt, [p15 (17) (17) (19) (19), tw3lt, k4, tw3rt] 3 times, p to end. **24th row:** As 8th row. **25th row:** P12 (12) (14) (14) (16), tw3lt, k2, tw3rt, [p17 (19) (19) (21) (21), tw3lt, k2, tw3rt] 3 times, p to end. **26th row:** As 6th row. **27th row:** P13 (13) (15) (15) (17), tw3lt, tw3rt, [p19 (21) (21) (23) (23), tw3lt, tw3rt] 3 times, p to end.
28th and 29th rows: As 2nd and 3rd rows. **30th row:** As 2nd row. ** Work a further 88 rows.
FOR ARMHOLES: Cast off 4 (5) (5) (6) (6) sts. at beginning of next 2 rows. Dec 1 st. each end of next 2 rows, then on the 2 following alternate rows – 91 (95) (99) (103) (107) sts. Work 58 (58) (62) (62) (66) rows.
FOR SHOULDERS: Cast off 29 (30) (31) (32) (33) sts at beginning of next 2 rows. Cast off 33 (35) (37) (39) (41) sts.

FRONT

Work as back to **. Work a further 87 rows.
DIVIDE FOR FRONT NECK: Next row: Pattern 51 (54) (56) (59) (61) and leave on a spare needle for right front neck, cast off 5 sts., pattern to end and work on remaining 51 (54) (56) (59)

(61) sts. for left front neck.

LEFT FRONT NECK: To shape armhole: Cast off 4 (5) (5) (6) (6) sts at beginning of next row. Pattern 1 row – omit this row when working right front neck. Dec 1 st at armhole edge on next 2 rows, then on the 2 following alternate rows - 43 (45) (47) (49) (51) sts. Work 31 (31) (35) (35) (39) rows – work 32 (32) (36) (36) (40) rows here when working right front neck.

TO SHAPE NECK: Next row: Cast off 6 (7) (8) (9) (10) sts., pattern to end. Dec 1 st. at neck edge on each of the next 5 rows, then on the 3 following alternate rows – 29 (30) (31) (32) (33) sts. Work 15 rows. Cast off for shoulder.

RIGHT FRONT NECK: With right side facing, rejoin m to inner end of sts on spare needle and pattern 1 row, then work as for left front neck, noting variations.

SLEEVES

With No. 10 (3¼ mm) needles and c cast on 41 (43) (45) (47) (49) sts. Work 25 rows in rib and colour sequence as given for back. continue with m only **Increase row:** Rib 2 (3) (4) (5) (6), inc., [rib 2, inc.] to last 2 (3) (4) (5) (6) sts, rib to end – 54 (56) (58) (60) (62) sts.

Change to No. 8 (4 mm) needles. **1st row (right side):** K4 (3) (4) (3) (4), p21 (23) (23) (25) (25), k4, p21 (23) (23) (25) (25), k4 (3) (4) (3) (4). **2nd row:** K and p to end, with sts as set. These 2 rows set position of pattern for the sleeves. Keeping continuity of pattern to match back, taking extra sts into pattern as they occur, work 2 rows, then inc 1 st each end of next row and the 12 (13) (12) (13) (12) following 6th (6th) (6th) (8th) (8th) rows – 80 (84) (84) (88) (88) sts. Work 33 (27) (33) (9) (17) rows.

SHAPE SLEEVE TOP: Cast off 4 (5) (5) (6) (6) sts at beginning of next 2 rows. Dec 1 st each end of next 2 rows and the 12 (11) (15) (14) (18) following alternate rows, then the next

12 (14) (10) (12) (8) rows. Cast off remaining 20 sts.

BUTTONHOLE/BUTTON BORDER

With right side facing, using No. 10 (3 mm) needles and m, pick up and k29 (29) (33) (33) (37) sts along straight row-ends of appropriate front edge. Beginning with an even-numbered row, work 3 rows in single rib as on back. **Buttonhole row:** With c, rib 3, work 2 tog, yf, [rib 8 (8) (10) (10) (12), work 2 tog, yf] twice, rib 4. Rib 1 row c, 2 rows m and 2 rows c. Cast off with c.
BUTTON BORDER: Work as buttonhole border, omitting buttonholes.

COLLAR

Using No. 10 (3¼ mm) needles and m, loosely cast on 103 (107) (111) (115) (119) sts and work 18 rows in rib as on back. Join in c and rib 2 rows c, 2 rows m and 2 rows c. Cast off loosely with c.

TO MAKE UP

Join shoulder seams. Set in sleeves. Join side and sleeve seams. Sew row-ends of buttonhole border to cast-off sts at centre front, then row-ends of button border behind buttonhole border. Add buttons. Sew on collar.

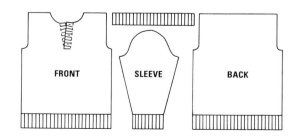

AUTUMN'S RICHES

THE SEASON'S MELLOW SHADES MAKE FOR A SUPER SWEATER FOR HIM

MEASUREMENTS To fit sizes 97 (102) (107) (112) cm/38 (40) (42) (44) in.

Actual measurement 111.5 (116.5) (121.5) (127) cm/43¾ (45¾) (47¾) (50) in.

Side seam All sizes 44 cm/17¼ in. **Length** 69 (70.5) (71) (72) cm/27¼ (27¾) (28) (28¼) in. **Sleeve seam** All sizes 51 cm/20 in.

MATERIALS

Allow following quantities in 100 g balls of Spectrum Detroit D.K.: 3 blue (French Navy 440), and 2 each in gold (Honey 414) and rust (Cognac 415) for 97 cm/38 in and 102 cm/40 in size; 4 blue and 2 each in gold and rust for 107 cm/42 in and 112 cm/44 in sizes. For any one size: No. 8 (4 mm) and No. 10 (3¼ mm) needles. Key: blue = bl, gold = g, rust = r.

For stockists, write to Spectrum Yarns Ltd, Spa Mills, New Street, Slaithwaite, Huddersfield HD7 5BB.

TENSION

23 stitches and 28 rows to measure 10 x 10 cm/4 x 4 in, over pattern, using No. 8 (4 mm) needles.

NOTE

Instructions are given for 97 cm/38 in size. Where they vary, work figures in round brackets for larger sizes. Instructions in square brackets are worked as stated after 2nd bracket.

BACK

With No. 10 (3¼ mm) needles and bl, cast on 116 (122) (128) (134) sts and work 19 rows in single rib. **Increase row:** Rib 9 (6) (9) (7), up1, [rib 9 (10) (10) (11), up1] to last 8 (6) (9) (6) sts, rib to end – 128 (134) (140) (146) sts. Change to No. 8 (4 mm) needles. Joining and breaking colours as required, work the 38-row pattern thus, twisting yarns when changing colours to avoid making a hole. **1st and 2nd rows:** All k with g. **3rd row:** All k with r. **4th row:** All p with r. **5th row:** K3 bl (2 r, 4 bl) (2 bl) (1 r, 4 bl), 3 r, [4 bl, 3 r] to last 3 (6) (2) (5) sts, 3 bl (4 bl, 2 r) (2 bl) (4 bl, 1 r). **6th row:** P nil (2 r, 1 bl) (1 r, 1 bl, 3 r, 1 bl) (1 r, 1 bl), 2 r, [1 bl, 3 r, 1 bl, 2 r] to last nil (3) (6) (2) sts, nil (1 bl, 2 r) (1 bl, 3 r, 1 bl, 1 r) (1 bl, 1 r). **7th row:** As 6th row. **8th row:** As 5th row. **9th and 10th rows:** As 3rd and 4th rows. **11th and 12th rows:** All k with g. **13th and 14th rows:** All k with bl. **15th row:** K1 g, [3 bl, 3 g] to last st, 1 bl. **16th row:** P2 bl, [3 g, 3 bl] to end. **17th row:** K2 bl, [3 g, 3 bl] to end. **18th row:** P1 g, [3 bl, 3 g] to last st, 1 bl. **19th row:** K1 r, [3 bl, 3 r] to last st, 1 bl. **20th row:** [P3 r, 3 bl] to last 2 sts, 2 r. **21st row:** [K3 r, 3 bl] to last 2 sts, 2 r. **22nd row:** 1 r, [3 bl, 3 r] to last st, 1 bl. **23rd and 24th rows:** All k with bl. **25th and 26th rows:** All k with r. **27th row:** All k with bl. **28th row:** All p with bl. **29th row:** K3 (2) (1) (4) bl, 1 g, [3 bl, 1 g] to last nil (3) (2) (5) sts, nil (3) (2) (5) bl. **30th row:** P3 (6) (1) (4) bl, 3 g, [5 bl, 3 g] to last 2 (5) (nil) (3) sts, 2 (5) (nil) (3) bl. **31st row:** K1 bl (4 bl) (1 g, 1 bl, 2 g, 3 bl) (2 bl), 2 g, 1 bl, 2 g, [3 bl, 2 g, 1 bl, 2 g] to last 2 (5) (nil) (3) sts, 2 (5) (nil) (3) bl. **32nd row:** Work to end with colours as set. 33rd row: K2 (5) (nil) (3) bl, 3 g, [5 bl, 3 g] to last 3 (6) (1) (4) st(s), 3 (6) (1) (4)

bl. **34th row:** P nil (3) (2) (5) bl, 1 g, [3 bl, 1 g] to last 3 (2) (1) (4) st(s), 3 (2) (1) (4) bl. **35th and 36th rows:** As 27th and 28th rows. **37th and 38th rows:** All k with r. Pattern a further 70 rows. Mark each end of last row, to denote end of side seams. ** Pattern a further 61 (65) (67) (69) rows.

DIVIDE FOR BACK NECK: Next row: Pattern 49 (51) (53) (55) and leave these sts on a spare needle for left back neck, cast off next 30 (32) (34) (36) sts, pattern to end and work on remaining 49 (51) (53) (55) sts for right back neck.

RIGHT BACK NECK: Dec 1 st at neck edge on each of next 4 (5) (5) (5) rows – 45 (46) (48) (50) sts. Pattern 4 (3) (3) (3) rows – pattern 5 (4) (4) (4) rows here when working left back neck.

FOR SHOULDER: Cast off 15 (15) (16) (17) sts at beginning of next row and the following alternate row – 15 (16) (16) (16) sts. Work 1 row. Cast off.

LEFT BACK NECK: With right side facing, rejoin appropriate yarn to inner end of sts on spare needle, and work as right back neck, noting variation.

FRONT

Work as given for back to **. Pattern a further 47 (51) (53) (55) rows.

DIVIDE FOR FRONT NECK: Next row: Pattern 56 (58) (60) (62) and leave these sts on a spare needle for right front neck, cast off next 16 (18) (20) (22) sts, pattern to end, and work on remaining 56 (58) (60) (62) sts for left front neck.

LEFT FRONT NECK: Dec 1 st at neck edge on each of next 11 (12) (12) (12) rows – 45 (46) (48) (50) sts. Pattern a further 11 (10) (10) (10) rows – pattern 12 (11) (11) (11) rows here when working right front neck.

FOR SHOULDER: Cast off 15 (15) (16) (17) sts at beginning of next row, and following alternate row – 15 (16) (16) (16) sts. Work 1 row. Cast off.

RIGHT FRONT NECK: With right side facing, rejoin appropriate yarn to inner end of sts on spare needle and work as left front neck, noting variation.

SLEEVES

With No. 10 (3¼ mm) needles and bl cast on 52 (54) (54) (56) sts and work 19 rows in single rib. **Increase row:** 4 (5) (8) (6), up1, [rib 4 (5) (3) (4), up1] to last 4 (4) (7) (6) sts, rib to end – 64 (64) (68) (68) sts. Change to No. 8 (4 mm) needles. Work pattern thus: **1st to 4th rows:** As 1st to 4th rows of back. **5th row:** K2 r (2 r) (1 bl, 3 r) (1 bl, 3 r), 4 bl, [3 r, 4 bl] to last 2 (2) (4) (4) sts, 2 r (2 r) (3 r, 1 bl) (3 r, 1 bl). **6th row:** P2 r (2 r) (1 bl, 3 r) (1 bl, 3 r), 1 bl, 2 r, 1 bl, [3 r, 1 bl, 2 r, 1 bl] to last 2 (2) (4) (4) sts, 2 r (2 r) (3 r, 1 bl) (3 r, 1 bl). **7th row:** As 6th row. **8th row:** As 5th row. **9th and 10th rows:** As 3rd and 4th rows. **11th (inc) row:** With g, inc, k until 1 st remains, inc – 66 (66) (70) (70) sts. **12th row:** All k with g. **13th and 14th rows:** All k with bl. **15th (inc) row:** Inc with g, k nil (nil) (2) (2) g, 3 bl, [3 g, 3 bl] to last 2 (2) (4) (4) sts, 1 (1) (3) (3) g, inc with g – 68 (68) (72) (72) sts. **16th row:** P1 (1) (3) (3) bl, [3 g, 3 bl] to last 1 (1) (3) (3) st(s), 1 (1) (3) (3) g. **17th row:** K nil (nil) (2) (2) g, [3 bl, 3 g] to last 2 (2) (4) (4) sts, 2 bl (2 bl) (3 bl, 1 g) (3 bl, 1 g). **18th row:** P nil (nil) (2) (2) g, [3 bl, 3 g] to last 2 (2) (4) (4) sts, 2 bl (2 bl) (3 bl, 1 g) (3 bl, 1 g). **19th (inc) row:** Inc with r (r) (bl) (bl), 1 (1) (3) (3) r, 3 bl, [3 r, 3 bl] to last 3 (3) (5) (5) sts, 2 r (2 r) (3 r, 1 bl) (3 r, 1 bl), inc with r (r) (bl) (bl) – 70 (70) (74) (74) sts. **20th row:** P nil (nil) (2) (2) bl, 3 r, [3 bl, 3 r] to last 1 (1) (3) (3) st(s), 1 (1) (3) (3) bl. **21st row:** K2 bl (2 bl) (1 r, 3 bl) (1 r, 3 bl), [3 r, 3 bl] to last 2 (2) (4) (4) sts, 2 r (2 r) (3 r, 1 bl) (3 r, 1 bl). **22nd row:** P1 (1) (3) (3) r, 3 bl, [3 r, 3 bl] to last nil (nil) (2) (2) sts, nil (nil) (2) (2) r. **23rd row:** With bl, inc, k to last st, inc – 72 (72) (76) (76) sts. **24th row:** All k with bl. **25th and 26th rows:** All k with r. **27th row:** With bl, inc, k to last st, inc – 74 (74) (78) (78) sts.

28th row: All p with bl. **29th row:** K nil (nil) (1 bl, 1 g) (1 bl, 1 g), [3 bl, 1 g] to last 2 (2) (nil) (nil) sts, 2 (2) (nil) (nil) bl. **30th row:** P1 (1) (3) (3) bl, [3 g, 5 bl] to last 1 (1) (3) (3) st(s), 1 (1) (3) (3) g. These 30 rows set position of pattern for the sleeves. Keeping continuity of pattern to match back, and working extra sts into pattern as they occur, inc 1 st at each end of next row, and 20 (22) (22) (23) following 4th rows – 116 (120) (124) (126) sts. Pattern a further 17 (9) (9) (5) rows. Cast off.

NECKBAND

Join right shoulder seam. With right side facing, rejoin bl and using No. 10 (3¼ mm) needles, pick up and k 24 sts from left front neck, 16 (18) (20) (22) sts across centre front, 24 sts from right front neck, 10 sts from right back neck, 30 (32) (34) (36) sts across centre back, and finally, 10 sts from left back neck – 114 (118) (122) (126) sts Work 24 rows in single rib. Cast off in rib.

TO MAKE UP

Do not press. Join left shoulder seam, continuing seam across neckband. Sew cast-off edge of sleeves to row-ends between markers on back and front. Join side and sleeve seams. Fold neckband in half to wrong side and lightly catch down.

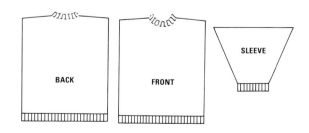

BACK

FRONT

SLEEVE

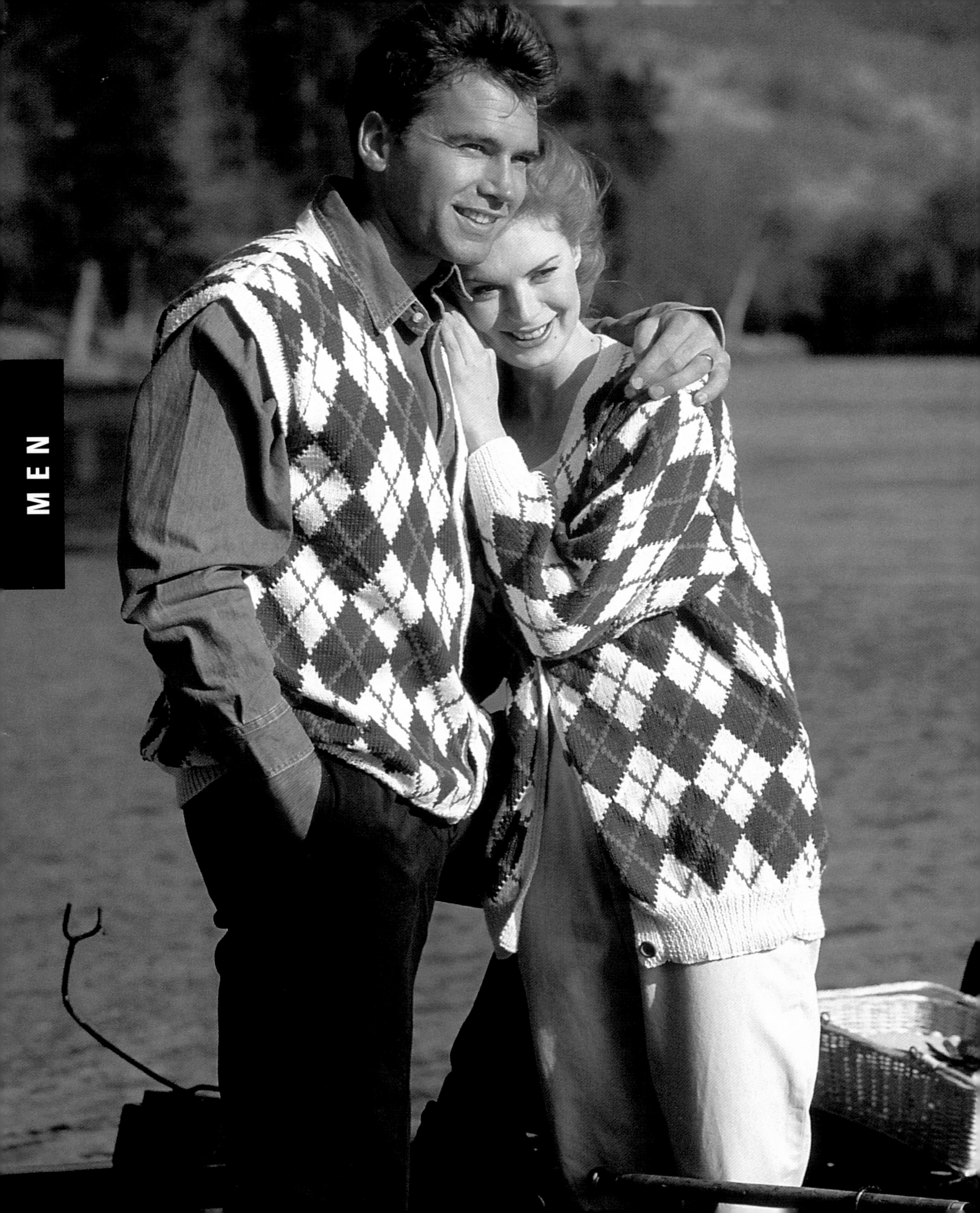

SCOTTISH STYLE

A DRAMATIC DOUBLE WITH A TRADITIONAL DIAMOND MOTIF

MEASUREMENTS To fit sizes 86-91 (97-102) (107-112) cm/34-36 (38-40) (42-44) in.

Actual measurement 112 (121) (130) cm/44 (47½) (51) in. **Cardigan side seam** All sizes 47 cm/18½ in.

Waistcoat side seam All sizes, including armhole border 49.5 cm/19½ in. **Length** All sizes 74 cm/29 in.

Cardigan sleeve seam All sizes 43 cm/17 in.

MATERIALS

CARDIGAN 8 (9) (10) 50 g balls of Jarol Body Talk D.K. in cream (Malibu 1808), 6 (6) (7) balls in navy (Indigo 1825) and 2 balls Raspberry (1820). WAISTCOAT 6 (7) (7) balls of same yarn in cream, 4 (5) (5) balls in navy and 1 (1) (2) balls Raspberry. For either design: No. 8 (4 mm) and No. 10 (3¼ mm) knitting needles; 6 buttons. Key: cream = c, navy = n.

For stockists, write to Jarol Ltd, White Rose Mills, Cape Street, Bradford BD1 4RN.

TENSION

22 stitches and 30 rows to 10 x 10 cm/4 x 4 in, over stocking stitch, using No. 8 (4 mm) needles.

NOTE

Instructions are given for 86-91 cm/34-36 in size. Where they vary, work figures in round brackets for larger sizes. Work instructions in square brackets as stated after 2nd bracket.

This cardigan, with matching waistcoat, has shallow set-in sleeves, and buttons to a V-neck. The bold diamond pattern is knitted in stocking stitch, using separate balls of yarn for each colour. The over-diamond is embroidered on afterwards. The yarn is machine-washable, cotton/acrylic D.K., with a crepe finish.

CARDIGAN
BACK

With No. 10 (3¼ mm) needles and c, cast on 101 (111) (121) sts, and beginning odd-numbered rows with k1 and even-numbered rows with p1, work 23 rows in single rib.
Increase row: Rib 2 (7) (3), inc, [rib 4 (4) (5), inc] to last 3 (8) (3) sts, rib to end – 121 (131) (141) sts.
Change to No. 8 (4 mm) needles. Using a separate ball of yarn for each colour section, work pattern, which is entirely in ss, beginning with a k row, so only colour details are given. When changing colours, twist yarns together to avoid leaving a hole. **1st and 2nd rows:** 10 (15) (10) c, 1n, [19c, 1n] to last 10 (15) (10) sts, 10 (15) (10) c. **3rd and 4th rows:** 9 (14) (9) c, 3n, [17c, 3n] to last 9 (14) (9) sts, 9 (14) (9) c. **5th and 6th rows:** 8 (13) (8) c, 5n, [15c, 5n] to last 8 (13) (8) sts, 8 (13) (8) c. **7th and 8th rows:** 7 (12) (7) c, 7n, [13c, 7n] to last 7 (12) (7) sts, 7 (12) (7) c. **9th and 10th rows:** 6 (11) (6) c, 9n, [11c, 9n] to last 6 (11) (6) sts, 6 (11) (6) c. **11th and 12th rows:** 5c (1n, 9c) (5c), 11n, [9c, 11n] to last 5 (10) (5) sts, 5c (9c, 1n) (5c). **13th and 14th rows:** 4c (2n, 7c) (4c), 13n, [7c, 13n] to last 4 (9) (4) sts, 4c (7c, 2n) (4c). **15th and 16th rows:** 3c (3n, 5c) (3c), 15n, [5c, 15n] to last 3 (8) (3) sts, 3c (5c, 3n) (3c). **17th and 18th rows:** 2c (4n, 3c) (2c), 17n, [3c, 17n] to last 2 (7) (2) sts, 2c (3c, 4n) (2c). **19th and 20th rows:** Nil (5) (nil) n, 1c, [19n, 1c] to last nil (5) (nil) sts, nil (5) (nil) n. **21st and 22nd rows:** All with n. **23rd to 40th rows:** Work 20th row back to 3rd row in that reverse order. These 40 rows form the pattern. Pattern another 82 rows.
FOR ARMHOLES: Dec 1 st each end of next 11 rows – 99 (109) (119) sts. Pattern 67 rows.
FOR SHOULDERS: Cast off 31 (34) (37) sts at beginning of next 2 rows. Cast off remaining 37 (41) (45) sts.

LEFT FRONT

With No. 10 (3¼ mm) needles cast on 49 (55) (59) sts and work 23 rows in rib as on back. **Increase row:** Rib 4, inc, [rib 3 (4) (4), inc] to last 4 (5) (4) sts, rib to end – 60 (65) (70) sts. Change to No. 8 (4 mm) needles, and place pattern thus: ** **1st pattern row:** 10 (15) (10) c, 1n, [19c, 1n] twice, 9 (9) (19) c. **2nd row:** Work to end with colours as set. ***.
Continuing in pattern to match back, pattern another 106 rows.
SHAPE FRONT EDGE: Dec 1 st at end – read beginning here when working right front – of next row and the 3 following 4th rows – 56 (61) (66) sts. Pattern 1 row.
FOR ARMHOLE: Dec 1 st at armhole edge on each of the next 11 rows, at same time, dec 1 st at front edge on 3rd of these rows and the 2 following 4th rows – 42 (47) (52) sts. Pattern 3 rows, then dec 1 st at front edge on next row and the 10 (12) (14) following 4th rows – 31 (34) (37) sts. Pattern 23 (15) (7) rows. Cast off remaining 31 (34) (37) sts straight across for shoulder.

RIGHT FRONT

Work as left front to **. **1st pattern row:** 9 (9) (19) c, 1n, [19c, 1n] twice, 10 (15) (10) c. **2nd row:** Work to end with colours as set. Work as left front from *** to end, noting variation.

SLEEVE

With No. 10 (3¼ mm) needles cast on 45 (49) (53) sts and work 23 rows in rib as on back. **Increase row:** Rib 7 (2) (5), inc, [rib 1 (3) (5), inc] to last 7 (2) (5) sts, rib to end – 61 sts.

Change to No. 8 (4 mm) needles and place pattern thus: **1st and 2nd rows:** 10c, 1n, [19c, 1n] twice, 10c. Keeping pattern correct to match back, and working extra sts into pattern as they occur, inc 1 st each end of next row and the 29 following 3rd rows – 121 sts. Pattern 20 rows.

SHAPE SLEEVE TOP: Dec 1 st each end of the next 11 rows. Cast off remaining 99 sts.

FRONT BAND

Join shoulder seams. With No. 10 (3¼ mm) needles cast on 11 sts and work 4 rows in rib as on back. **1st buttonhole row:** Rib 4, cast off 3 sts, rib to end. **2nd buttonhole row:** Rib to end, casting on 3 sts over those cast off in previous row. Rib 22 rows. Repeat last 24 rows, 4 times more, then the 2 buttonhole rows again. Continue in rib until band fits up remainder of appropriate front, round back neck and down other front, casting off when correct length is assured.

TO MAKE UP

Press as given on ball band. Set sleeves into armholes matching shapings. Join side and sleeve seams. Sew front band into place, setting top buttonhole level with first front dec. Add buttons.

FOR EMBROIDERY: Along 1st pattern row of each section, place markers on cream st mid-way between navy sts – 10th st of cream section. Using these marked sts as starting points, Swiss embroider over diamonds with Raspberry, moving 1 st over every 2 rows.

(Swiss embroidery is a simple technique, using a contrast coloured yarn to embroider the surface of plain stocking stitch by imitating and covering each knitted stitch with the contrast yarn.) Continue all over to top.

WAISTCOAT

Work back, fronts and front band as cardigan.

ARMHOLE BORDERS

With right side facing, rejoin c, and using No. 10 (3¼ mm) needles, pick up and k 131 sts all round armhole edge. Work 9 rows in rib as on back, decreasing 1 st each end of 1st row and every alternate row. Cast off in rib. Join side seams, including borders. Complete and work embroidery as on cardigan.

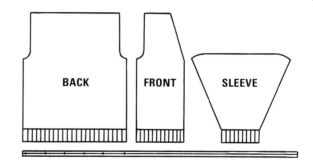

BACK   FRONT   SLEEVE

LITTLE

CHARMER

———

HE'LL ALWAYS BE WARM IN THIS POCKET-SIZED WAISTCOAT

MEASUREMENTS To fit sizes 61 (66) (71) (76) (81) cm/24 (26) (28) (30) (32) in.

Actual measurement 66 (72) (78) (84) (89.5) cm/26 (28¼) (30¾) (33) (35¼) in.

Side seam including borders 28 (29.5) (31) (32) (33.5) cm/11 (11½) (12¼) (12½) (13) in.

Length 42 (44.5) (47.5) (50) (53) cm/16½, (17½) (18¾) (19¾) (20¾) in.

MATERIALS
2 (2) (2) (3) (3) 100 g balls of House of Fraser Classic D.K.; No.8 (4 mm) and No.10 (3¼ mm) knitting needles; a No. 10 (3¼ mm) circular knitting needle; 4 buttons. Yarn used: Natural.

TENSION
27 stitches and 29 rows, to measure 10 x 10 cm/4 x 4 in, over the pattern, using No. 8 (4 mm) needles.

NOTE
Instructions are given for the 61 cm/24 in size. where they vary, work figures in round brackets for larger sizes. Instructions in square brackets are worked as stated after 2nd bracket.

This classic waistcoat has curved armholes, set-in pockets, and pointed fronts. It is knitted in simple, wide-twist rib, with easy-to-work mitred front corners. The yarn is machine-washable, acrylic wool/nylon D.K.

BACK

With No. 10 (3¼ mm) needles cast on 85 (93) (101) (109) (117) sts and, beginning odd-numbered rows with k1 and even-numbered rows with p1, work 6 rows in single rib, increasing 4 sts evenly across last row – 89 (97) (105) (113) (121) sts.
Change to No. 8 (4 mm) needles. Work the 2-row pattern thus: **1st row:** P2, k1b, [p3, k1b] to last 2 sts, p2. **2nd row:** K2, p1b, [k3, p1b] to last 2 sts, k2.
Pattern another 68 (72) (76) (80) (84) rows.
FOR ARMHOLES: Keeping continuity of pattern, cast off 4 (5) (6) (7) (8) sts at beginning of next 2 rows, then dec 1 st each end of next 7 (8) (9) (10) (11) rows – 67 (71) (75) (79) (83) sts. Pattern 35 (38) (41) (44) (47) rows.
FOR SHOULDERS: Cast off 20 (22) (23) (25) (26) sts at beginning of next 2 rows. Leave remaining 27 (27) (29) (29) (31) sts on a spare needle.

POCKET LININGS

Make 2 pocket linings. With No. 8 (4 mm) needles cast on 17 (17) (21) (21) (25) sts and beginning with a p row, rss 20 rows. Leave sts on a st holder.

LEFT FRONT

With No. 8 (4 mm) needles cast on 3 sts.
1st row (right side): All p. **2nd row:** Cast on 3 sts, k these 3 sts, p1b, k2. **3rd row:** Cast on 5 (6)

(7) (8) (9) sts, then nil (k1b) (p1, k1b) (p2, k1b) (p3, k1b), p3, k1b, p1 across these sts, p2, k1b, p3.**4th row:** Cast on 3 sts, k2, p1b across these sts, k3, p1b, k3, p1b, k3, then nil (p1b) (p1b, k1) (p1b, k2) (p1b, k3).
These 4 rows set pattern. Keeping continuity of pattern, taking extra sts into pattern as they occur, continue thus: **5th row:** Cast on 5 (6) (7) (8) (9) sts, pattern to end. **6th row:** Cast on 3 sts, pattern to end. **7th to 10th rows:** Repeat 5th and 6th rows, twice.
Cast on 4 sts at beginning of next row – 42 (46) (50) (54) (58) sts. Pattern 17 rows.
Pocket row: Pattern 11 (13) (13) (15) (15), sl next 17 (17) (21) (21) (25) sts on to a st holder and leave at front. In their place, pattern 17 (17) (21) (21) (25) sts of one pocket lining, pattern to end. Pattern 51 (55) (59) (63) (67) rows.
FOR ARMHOLE AND TO SHAPE NECK: 1st row: Cast off 4 (5) (6) (7) (8) sts, pattern to last 2 sts, dec. **2nd row:** Pattern to end.
** Dec 1 st at armhole edge on next 7 (8) (9) (10) (11) rows, at the same time, dec 1 st at neck edge on 2nd of these rows and the 1 (2) (2) (2) (3) following 3rd row(s) – 28 (29) (31) (33) (34) sts.
Keeping armhole edge straight, pattern nil (2) (1) (nil) (2) row(s), then dec 1 st at neck edge on next row and 7 (6) (7) (7) (7) following 3rd rows – 20 (22) (23) (25) (26) sts. Pattern 13 (17) (18) (22) (23) rows – pattern 14 (18) (19) (23) (24) rows here when working right front. Cast off for shoulder.

RIGHT FRONT

With No. 8 (4 mm) needles cast on 3 sts.
1st row (right side): All p. **2nd row:** Cast on 5 (6) (7) (8) (9) sts, then nil (p1b) (k1, p1b) (k2, p1b) (k3, p1b), k3, p1b, k1 across these sts, k2, p1b.**3rd row:** Cast on 3 sts, p these sts, k1b, p3, k1b, p3, then nil (k1b) (k1b, p1) (k1b, p2) (k1b, p3).

These 3 rows set pattern. Keeping continuity of pattern, taking extra sts into pattern as they occur, continue thus: **4th row:** Cast on 5 (6) (7) (8) (9) sts, pattern to end. **5th row:** Cast on 3 sts, pattern to end. **6th to 9th rows:** Repeat 4th and 5th rows, twice. **11th row:** Cast on 4 sts at beginning of next row, and 3 sts on following row – 42 (46) (50) (54) (58) sts. Pattern 17 rows.

Pocket row: Pattern 14 (16) (16) (18) (18), sl next 17 (17) (21) (21) (25) sts on to a st holder and leave at front. In their place, pattern 17 (17) (21) (21) (25) sts of other pocket lining, pattern to end. Pattern 51 (55) (59) (63) (67) rows.

FOR ARMHOLE AND TO SHAPE NECK: 1st row: Dec, pattern to end. **2nd row:** Cast off 4 (5) (6) (7) (8) sts, pattern to end. Work as left front from ** to end, noting variation.

ARMHOLE BORDERS

Join shoulder seams. With right side facing, using No. 10 (3¼ mm) needles, pick up and k80 (90) (100) (110) (120) sts around armhole edge and work 6 rows in single rib. Cast off in rib.

FRONT BORDER

With right side facing, using No. 10 (3¼ mm) circular needle, beginning at side edge of right front, pick up and k24 (30) (34) (40) (44) sts to point at cast-on edge, 1 st from point, mark this st, pick up and k17 sts to point, 1 st from point, mark this st, pick up and k54 (58) (62) (66) (70) sts to first front dec, 34 (38) (42) (46) (50) sts to shoulder, k27 (27) (29) (29) (31) sts at back neck dec 2 sts evenly, pick up and k34 (38) (42) (46) (50) sts to first front dec, 54 (58) (62) (66) (70) sts to point, 1 st from point, mark this st, pick up and k17 sts to point at cast-on edge, 1 st from point, mark this st, then pick up and k24 (30) (34) (40) (44) sts to side edge of left front – 287 (315) (341) (369) (395) sts.

Working backwards and forwards in rows, continue thus: **1st row:** *** then * P1, k1 *; work from * to * to marked st, up1, p1, up1, k1; work from *** 3 times more, then from * to * to last st, p1.
Rib 1 row, increasing as before.

1st buttonhole row: Rib 52 (58) (62) (68) (72), increasing as before, cast off 2 sts, [rib a further 12 (13) (15) (17) (19), cast off 2 sts] 3 times, rib to end, increasing as before.

2nd buttonhole row: Rib to end, casting on 2 sts over each cast off group in previous row, increasing as before. Rib 2 rows, increasing as before. Cast off in rib.

POCKET TOPS

With right side facing, using No. 10 (3¼ mm) needles, rejoin yarn to 17 (17) (21) (21) (25) sts on st holder and work 6 rows in rib as given on back. Cast off in rib.

TO MAKE UP

Press as given on ball band. Join side seams. Catch pocket linings to wrong side and row-ends of pocket tops to right side. Add buttons.

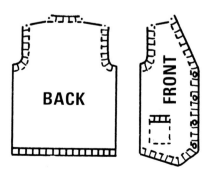

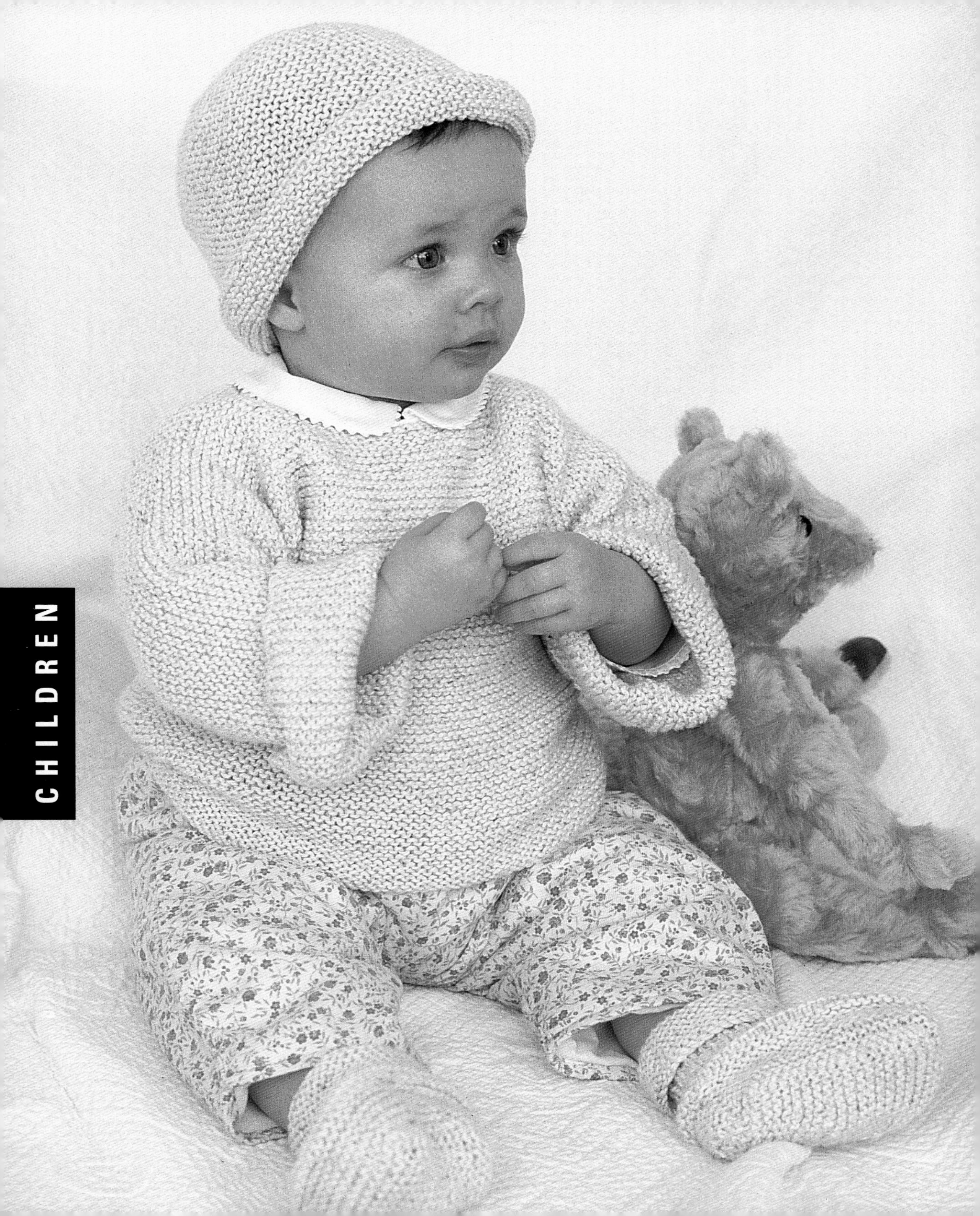

SWEET AND EASY

Baby's all set to go in matching top, pull-on hat and bootees

MEASUREMENTS: SWEATER To fit sizes 46 (51) (56) cm/18 (20) (22) in. **Actual measurement** 54 (57.5) (61) cm/21 (22½) (24) in.
Side seam 15 (16) (17) cm/6 (6¼) (6½) in. **Length from centre neck** 23.5 (25.5) (27.5) cm/9¼ (10) (10¾) in.
Sleeve seam with cuff turned back 14 (16) (17.5) cm/5½ (6¼) (7) in. **HAT** All round at widest part 31.5 (34.5) (37) cm/12½ (13½) (14½) in.
BOOTEES Foot length 12.5 (14) (15) cm/5 (5½) (6) in.

MATERIALS
SWEATER: 4 (4) (5) 50 g balls of Hayfield Raw Cotton Classics Tweed D.K.
HAT AND BOOTEES: 2 (3) (3) balls. For any one size of garment; No. 9 (3¾ mm) and No. 10 (3¼ mm) knitting needles. Yarn used: Wheatsheaf (055). For stockists, write to Hayfield Textiles Ltd, Glusburn, Keighley, West Yorkshire BD20 8QP.

TENSION
23 stitches and 43 rows, to 10 x 10 cm/4 x 4 in, over the garter stitch, using No. 9 (3¾ mm) needles.

NOTE
Instructions are given for the 46 cm/18 in size. Where they vary work figures in round brackets for larger sizes. Work instructions in square brackets as stated after the 2nd bracket.

This garter-stitch top is knitted in one piece with turning rows for the neck shaping, and the matching pull-on hat has a turn-back brim. The bootees have an easy-to-work ridge knitted in. The yarn is machine-washable, raw cotton tweed D.K.

SWEATER
BACK, FRONT AND SLEEVES

The back, front and sleeves are worked in one piece. With No. 10 (3¼ mm) needles cast on 62 (66) (70) sts for lower edge of back and beginning with a wrong side row, gst 7 rows. Change to No. 9 (3¾ mm) needles and gst a further 58 (62) (66) rows.
FOR SLEEVES: Cast on 44 (48) (52) sts at beginning of each of the next 2 rows – 150 (162) (174) sts.
Gst a further 34 (38) (42) rows.
** TO SHAPE 1ST SIDE OF BACK NECK: 1st and 2nd turning rows: K71 (75) (79) sts, turn for 1st row, sl1, then k to end for 2nd row.
3rd and 4th turning rows: K68 (72) (76) sts, turn for 3rd row, sl1, then k to end for 4th row.
5th and 6th turning rows: K66 (70) (74) sts, turn for 5th row, sl1, then k to end for 6th row.
7th and 8th turning rows: K64 (68) (72) sts, turn for 7th row, sl1, then k to end for 8th row.
9th and 10th turning rows: K63 (67) (71) sts, turn for 9th row, sl1, then k to end for 10 th row.
11th and 12th turning rows: K62 (66) (70) sts, turn for 11th row, sl1, then k to end for 12th row. ** **Next row:** K across all sts.
TO SHAPE 2ND SIDE OF BACK NECK: Work as for 1st side of back neck from ** to **.
K 2 rows across all sts. **Next row:** K61 (65) (69) sts, cast off next 28 (32) (36) sts kwise for centre back neck, k to end. **Next row:** K61 (65) (69) sts, cast on 28 (32) (36) sts for centre front neck, k to end – 150 (162) (174) sts. K 2 rows.
*** TO SHAPE 1ST SIDE OF FRONT NECK: 1st and 2nd turning rows: K62 (66) (70) sts, turn for 1st row, sl1, then k to end for 2nd row.
3rd and 4th turning rows: K63 (67) (71) sts, turn for 3rd row, sl1, then k to end for 4th row.
5th and 6th turning rows: K64 (68) (72) sts, turn for 5th row, sl1, then k to end for 6th row.
7th and 8th turning rows: K66 (70) (74) sts, turn for 7th row, sl1, then k to end for 8th row.
9th and 10th turning rows: K68 (72) (76) sts, turn for 9th row, sl1, then k to end for 10th row.
11th and 12th turning rows: K71 (75) (79) sts, turn for 11th row, sl1, then k to end for 12th row. *** K 1 row across all sts.
TO SHAPE 2ND SIDE OF FRONT NECK: Work as for 1st side of front neck from *** to ***.
Gst 34 (38) (42) rows across all sts.
FOR SLEEVES: Cast off 44 (48) (52) sts at the beginning of each of the next 2 rows – 62 (66) (70) sts. Gst a further 58 (62) (66) rows.
Change back to No. 10 (3¼ mm) needles and gst a further 7 rows. Cast off.

TO COMPLETE: Do not press. Join side and underarm seams, reversing seam for 5 cm/2 in cuff. Fold cuffs over to right side.

HAT

With No. 9 (3¾ mm) needles cast on 85 (92) (97) sts for brim and gst 59 (63) (67) rows, ending with a wrong-side row.
TO SHAPE FOR CROWN: 1st (dec) row: K1, [k2tog, k5 (k2tog, k5) (k2tog, k6)] to end – 73 (79) (85) sts. Gst 5 rows. **2nd (dec) row:** K1, [k2tog, k4] to end – 61 (66) (71) sts. Gst 3 rows. **3rd (dec) row:** K1, [k2tog, k3] to end – 49 (53) (57) sts. Gst 3 rows. **4th (dec) row:** K1, [k2tog, k2] to end – 37 (40) (43) sts. Gst 3 rows. **5th (dec) row:** K1, [k2tog, k1] to end - 25 (27) (29) sts. Gst 1 row.
6th (dec) row: K1, [k2tog] to end – 13 (14) (15) sts.

TO COMPLETE: Break off yarn, leaving a long end, thread this through remaining sts, draw up tightly and secure. Join back seam, reversing seam for approximately 10 (11) (12) cm/4 (4½) (4¾) in for foldback. Fold brim over to right side.

BOOTEES

With No. 10 (3¼ mm) needles cast on 38 (42) (46) sts and beginning with a right side row, gst 8 rows.
Change to No. 9 (3¾ mm) needles and gst a further 8 rows. Work 10 rows in single rib. Gst a further 6 rows.
SHAPE INSTEP:
Next row: K25 (27) (29) sts, turn and leave remaining 13 (15) (17) sts on a spare needle.
Next row: K12 sts, turn and leave remaining 13 (15) (17) sts on a spare needle. Working on centre 12 sts for instep, gst 16 (20) (24) rows.
Break off yarn and leave sts on a st holder. With right side of work facing, rejoin yarn to base of instep, pick up and k 10 (11) (12) sts from row-ends of one side of instep, k across the 12 sts of instep, pick up and k 10 (11) (12) sts from row-ends of other side of instep, k 13 (15) (17) from spare needle – 58 (64) (70) sts. Gst 8 rows.
Next (wrong side) ridge row: [Pick up 1 st 7 rows down from corresponding st on left-hand needle, sl it on to left-hand needle, then k it tog with next st on left-hand needle] to end. Gst 10 rows. Break off yarn.
SHAPE SOLE: With right side of work facing, sl first 22 (25) (28) sts on to right-hand needle, rejoin yarn to remaining sts and work thus:
1st row: K13, k2tog, turn. **2nd row:** Sl1, k12, k2togb, turn. **3rd row:** Sl1, k12, k2tog, turn. Repeat 2nd and 3rd rows, 8 (10) (12) times more, then the 2nd row again. Continue thus:
1st row: Sl1, k4, k2togb, k2tog, k4, k2tog, turn. **2nd row:** Sl1, k10, k2togb, turn. **3rd row:** Sl1, k10, k2tog, turn. Repeat 2nd and 3rd rows, once, then the 2nd row again. **7th row:**

Sl1, k3, k2togb, k2tog, k3, k2tog, turn. **8th row:** Sl1, k8, k2togb, turn. **9th row:** Sl1, k8, k2tog, turn. Repeat 8th and 9th rows, 3 (4) (5) times.
Next row: Sl1, k2, k2togb, k2tog, k2, k2togb, turn.
Sl 8 sts of sole on to a spare needle, place remaining 4 sts at each side on to a separate needle and place behind sole sts, then with wrong side facing, working through both sets of sts, cast them off tog.

TO COMPLETE: Join seam, reversing seam for foldback. Fold cuff over to right side.

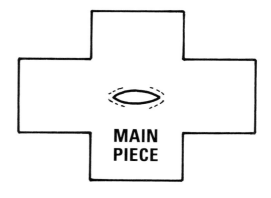

BOY BLUE

BRIGHT AND BREEZY IN A SUMMER-WEIGHT COTTON JERSEY

MEASUREMENTS To fit sizes 51 (56) (61) (66) cm/20 (22) (24) (26) in.

Actual measurement 58.5 (64.5) (67.5) (73.5) cm/23 (25¼) (26½) (29) in. **Side seam** 19.5 (21) (22.5) (23.5) cm/7¾ (8¼) (8¾) (9¼) in.

Length 34 (37) (39.5) (42.5) cm/13¼ (14½) (15½) (16¾) in. **Sleeve seam** 24.5 (25.5) (27) (29) cm/9½ (10) (10½) (11½) in.

MATERIALS

4 (5) (6) (7) 50 g balls of Stylecraft Soft Cotton D.K. in blue (Burmuda Blue 5116) and 1 ball each in green (Spearmint 5111) and white (5001); No. 8 (4 mm) and No. 10 (3¼ mm) knitting needles; a cable needle.
Key: blue = bl, green = gr, white = w.
For stockists, write to Stylecraft, P.O. Box 62, Goulbourne Street, Keighley, West Yorkshire BD21 1PP.

TENSION

27 stitches and 29 rows, to 10 x 10 cm/4 x 4 in, over main pattern and border pattern of 9 rows, to measure 3.5 cm/3⅜ in depth, using No. 8 (4 mm) needles.

NOTE

Instructions are given for 51 cm/20 in size. Where they vary, work figures in round brackets for larger sizes. Work instructions in square brackets as stated after 2nd bracket.

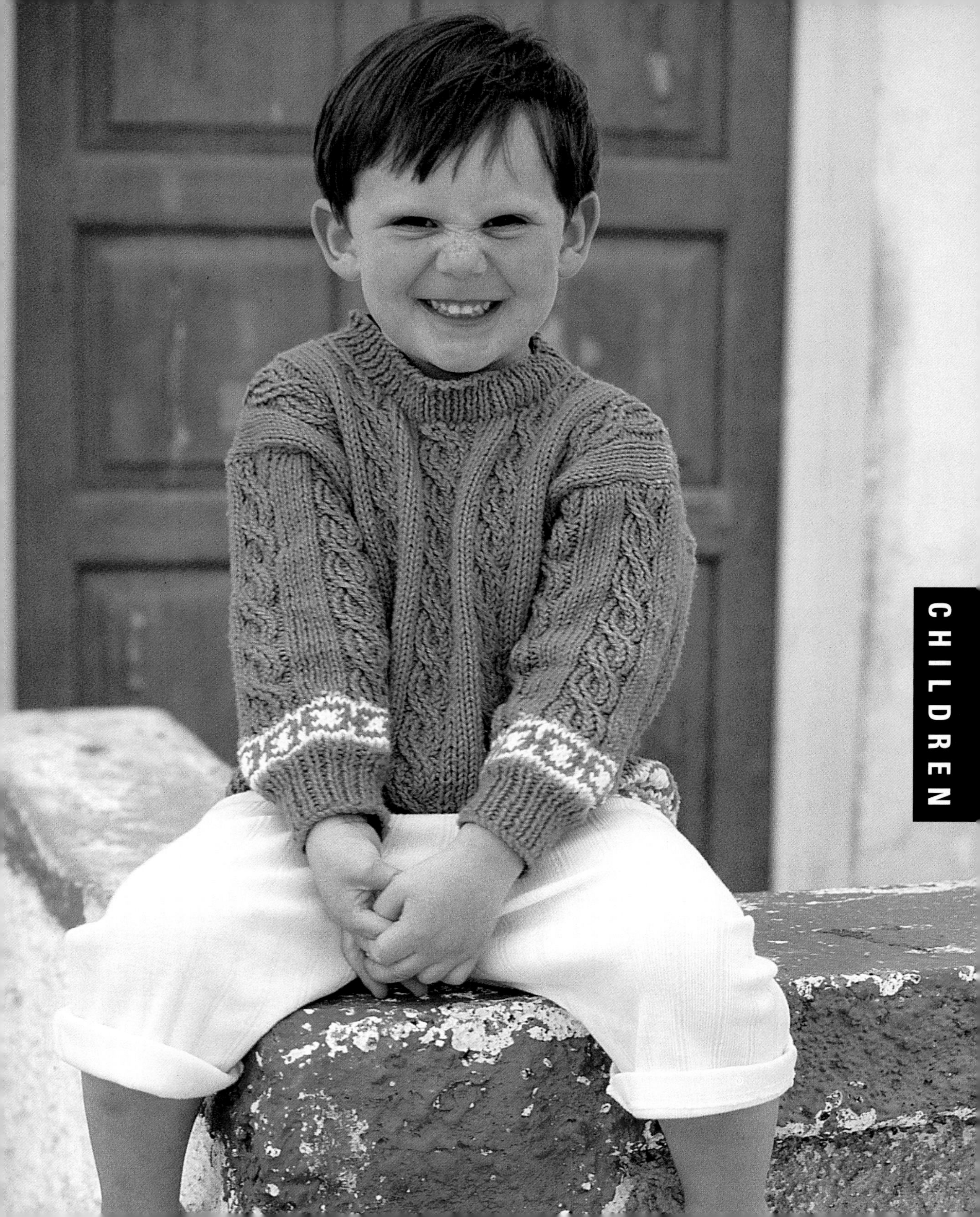

A casual-style sweater that features dropped shoulders and a round neck. The pattern is twist-rib cable panels, with three-colour borders. The cuffs and neck are finished with single rib. The yarn is soft cotton D.K.

BACK

With No. 10 (3¼ mm) needles and gr, cast on 74 (78) (86) (94) sts and work in fancy rib thus: **1st row:** All k. **2nd row:** P2, [k2, p2] to end. Break off gr. Keeping yarn not in use at wrong side of work, continue in rib thus: **3rd row:** K2bl, [2w, 2bl] to end. **4th row:** P2bl, [k2w, p2bl] to end. Repeat 3rd and 4th rows, twice more.

Change to No. 8 (4 mm) needles, then joining in and breaking off colours as required, work the border pattern, which is worked in ss beginning with a k row, so only the colour details are given. Avoid drawing yarn too tightly across back and when changing colours, wind yarn round the one just used, to avoid leaving a gap. **1st row:** All gr. 2nd row: All w. **3rd row:** 5 (nil) (4) (1) bl, 1w, [6bl, 1w] to last 5 (nil) (4) (1) st(s), 5 (nil) (4) (1) bl. **4th row:** 4w, 1bl, 1w (1w) (3w, 1bl, 1w) (1bl, 1w), [1bl, 4w, 1bl, 1w] to last 5 (nil) (4) (1) st(s), 1bl, 4w (nil) (1bl, 3w) (1bl). **5th row:** 1 (3) (nil) (4) bl, 2w, [5bl, 2w] to last 1 (3) (nil) (4) sts, 1 (3) (nil) (4) bl. **6th to 9th rows:** As 4th row back to 1st row, in that reverse order. Continue in bl only.

Increase row: P9 (7) (9) (9), inc, [p13 (7) (16) (18), inc] to last 8 (6) (8) (8) sts, p to end – 79 (87) (91) (99) sts. Work 8-row main pattern thus: **1st row:** K2 (6) (6) (8), p1, cr4rt, p1, cr4lt, p1, [k5 (5) (6) (7), p1, cr4rt, p1, cr4lt, p1] to last 2 (6) (6) (8) sts, k to end. **2nd row:** P2 (6) (6) (8), [k1, p1b] twice, k3, [p1b, k1] twice, [p5 (5) (6) (7), k1, p1b, k1, p1b, k3, p1b, k1, p1b, k1] to last 2 (6) (6) (8) sts, p to end. **3rd row:** K2 (6) (6) (8), [p1,

k1b] twice, p3, [k1b, p1] twice, [k5 (5) (6) (7), p1, k1b, p1, k1b, p3, k1b, p1, k1b, p1] to last 2 (6) (6) (8) sts, k to end. **4th row:** As 2nd row. **5th row:** K2 (6) (6) (8), p1, cr4lt, p1, cr4rt, p1, [k5 (5) (6) (7), p1, cr4lt, p1, cr4rt, p1] to last 2 (6) (6) (8) sts, k to end. **6th row:** P2 (6) (6) (8), k2, [p1b, k1] 3 times, p1b, k2, [p5 (5) (6) (7), k2, p1b, k1, p1b, k1, p1b, k1, p1b, k2] to last 2 (6) (6) (8) sts, p to end. **7th row:** K2 (6) (6) (8), p2, cr7, p2, [k5 (5) (6) (7), p2, cr7, p2] to last 2 (6) (6) (8) sts, k to end. **8th row:** As 6th row. These 8 rows form the main pattern. Pattern 30 (34) (38) (42) rows. Mark each end of the last row for end of side seams. Pattern a further 40 (44) (48) (52) rows.

FOR SHOULDERS: Cast off 23 (25) (26) (29) sts at the beginning of each of the next 2 rows. Leave 33 (37) (39) (41) sts.

FRONT

Work as for back to markers. Pattern a further 25 (29) (33) (37) rows.

DIVIDE FOR FRONT NECK: Next row: Pattern 32 (34) (35) (38) and leave these sts for right front neck, pattern the next 15 (19) (21) (23) and leave these sts on a st holder, pattern to end and work on last 32 (34) (35) (38) sts for left front neck.

LEFT FRONT NECK: Dec 1 st at neck edge on next 5 rows and then on the 4 following alternate rows – 23 (25) (26) (29) sts. Pattern 1 row – pattern 2 rows here for right front neck. Cast off for shoulder.

RIGHT FRONT NECK: With right side facing, rejoin bl to sts on spare needle and work as for left front neck, noting variation.

SLEEVES

With No. 10 (3¼ mm) needles and bl, cast on 35 (37) (39) (41) sts and, beginning odd-numbered rows with k1 and even-numbered

rows with p1, work 13 rows in single rib.
Increase row: Rib 2 (1) (5) (4), inc, [rib 2 (2) (1) (1), inc] to last 2 (2) (5) (4) sts, rib 2 (rib 1, inc) (rib 5) (rib 4) – 46 (50) (54) (58) sts.

Change to No. 8 (4 mm) needles. Work border pattern thus: **1st row:** All gr. 2nd row: All w. **3rd row:** 5 (nil) (2) (4) bl, 1w, [6bl, 1w] to last 5 (nil) (2) (4) st(s), 5 (nil) (2) (4) bl. **4th row:** 4w (1w, 1bl, 4w) (1w) (3w), [1bl, 1w, 1bl, 4w] to last nil (2) (4) (6) sts, nil (1bl, 1w) (1bl, 1w, 1bl, 1w) (1bl, 1w, 1bl, 3w). These 4 rows place border pattern. Work remaining 5 rows of border pattern to match back. **Increase row:** P5 (5) (5) (4), inc, [p2 (3) (3) (4), inc] to last 4 (4) (4) (3) sts, p to end – 59 (61) (66) (69) sts. Place main pattern thus: **1st row:** K nil (1) (2) (2), p1, cr4rt, p1, cr4lt, p1, [k5 (5) (6) (7), p1, cr4rt, p1, cr4lt, p1] to last nil (1) (2) (2) sts, k to end. This row places main pattern for sleeves. Keeping continuity of main pattern to match back, pattern a further 3 rows. Continuing in pattern to match back and taking extra sts into ss as they occur, inc 1 st at each end of the next row and the 7 (8) (9) (12) following 4th rows – 75 (79) (86) (95) sts. Pattern 13 (13) (13) (7) rows. Cast off.

NECKBAND

Join right shoulder seam. With right side facing and using No. 10 (3¼ mm) needles and bl, pick up and k17 sts down left front neck, k the 15 (19) (21) (23) sts at centre, pick up and k17 sts up right front neck, then k the 33 (37) (39) (41) sts at back neck – 82 (90) (94) (98) sts. Work 7 rows in single rib. Cast off in rib.

TO MAKE UP

Press as given on ball band. Join left shoulder seam, including neckband. Sew cast-off edge of sleeves between markers on back and front. Join sleeve and side seams.

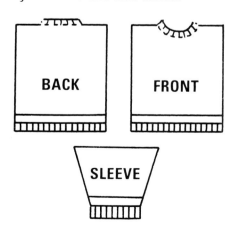

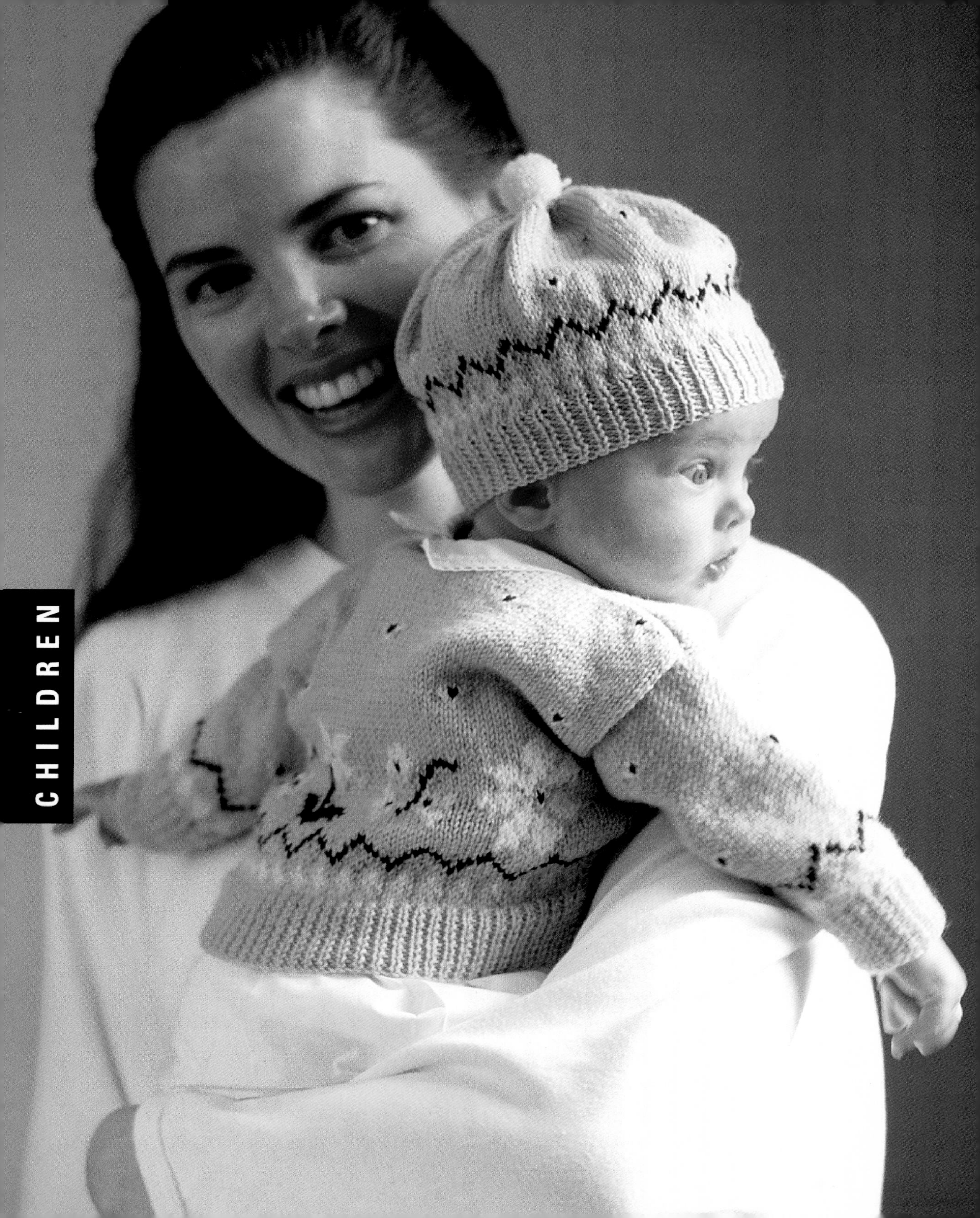

BABY

GRAND

THIS SUPER SET'S THE TOPS FOR TINY TOTS

MEASUREMENTS To fit sizes 0-3 months (3-6 months) **CARDIGAN Actual measurements** 48.5 (53.5) cm/19 (21) in.
Side seam 13.5 (15) cm/5¼ (6) in. **Length** 24.5 (27) cm/9½ (10½) in. **Sleeve seam** 17.5 (19.5) cm/6¾ (7½) in.
HAT All round widest part 45 cm/17¾ in.

MATERIALS
3-50 g balls of Jaeger Merino Baby 4 ply in Sky (48) and 1 ball each in Buttermilk (46), white (45) and navy (Indigo 44), a pair of No. 10 (3¼ mm) and No. 12 (2¾ mm) knitting needles; 7 buttons. Key: Sky = s, Buttermilk = m, white = w, navy = n.
For stockists, write to Coats Patons Crafts, McMullen Road, Darlington, Co. Durham DL1 1YQ

TENSION
31 stitches and 35 rows, to measure 10 x 10 cm/4 x 4 in, over pattern, using No. 10 (3¼ mm) knitting needles.

NOTE
Instructions are given for 0-3 months size. Where they vary, work figures in round brackets for larger size. Instructions in square brackets are worked as stated after 2nd bracket.

This cardigan is knitted mainly in stocking stitch with ribbed borders, it has contrast chevron bands, all-over diamond pattern and a border of flowers. The yarn is machine-washable, luxurious pure wool baby 4-ply.

CARDIGAN
MAIN PART

Main part of cardigan is worked in one piece to end of motifs. With No. 12 (3¾ mm) needles and s cast on 143 (159) sts and, beginning odd-numbered rows with k1 and even-numbered rows with p1, single rib 17 rows.

Change to No. 10 (3¼ mm) needles. Use small separate balls for each colour section. Work border pattern, which is in ss, beginning with a k row, so only colour details are given. **1st and 2nd rows:** All s. **3rd row:** 3s, [1m, 3s] to end. **4th row:** 1m, 1s, [3m, 1s] to last st, 1m. **5th row:** As 3rd row. **6th row:** All s. **7th row:** 7s, [1n, 7s] to end. **8th row:** 1n, 5s, 1n, [1s, 1n, 5s, 1n] to end. **9th row:** 1s, 1n, [3s, 1n] to last st, 1s. **10th row:** 2 s, 1n, 1s, 1n, [5s, 1n, 1s, 1n] to last 2 sts, 2s. **11th row:** 3s, 1n, [7s, 1n] to last 3 sts, 3s. **12th row:** All s. **PLACE MOTIFS: 1st row:** 8 (11)s, for chart B 1n, 36 (39)s, for chart A 1w, 5s, 1w, 28 (31)s, for chart B 1n, 35 (39)s, for chart A 1w, 5s, 1w, 20 (23)s. Reading even-numbered rows from left to right, and odd- numbered rows from right to left, work 2nd to 19th rows following charts. **Dividing row:** With s, p34 (38), leave for left front, p75 (83), leave for back, p last 34 (38), leave for right front.

BACK: Rejoin yarn to sts. Ss 2 rows s. Mark each end of last row for 1st size. Work dot pattern thus: **1st row:** 22 (26)s, 1m, 29s, 1m, 22 (26)s. **2nd row:** 21 (25)s, 1m, 1n, 1m, 27s, 1m, 1n, 1m, 21 (25)s. **3rd row:** As 1st row. **4th to 10th rows:** All s, marking each end of 1st of these rows for 2nd size. **11th row:** 7 (11) s, 1m, [29s, 1m] twice – 7 (11)s. **12th row:** 6 (10)s, 1m, 1n, 1m, [27s, 1m, 1n, 1m] twice, 6 (10)s. **13th row:** As 11th row. **14th to 20th rows:** All s. Work another 16 (24) rows. **FOR SHOULDERS:** Cast off 21 (24) sts. at start of next 2 rows. Leave 33 (35) sts.

LEFT FRONT: Rejoin yarns to inner end of left front sts. Ss 2 rows s. Mark end of last row for 1st size. Place dot pattern thus: **1st row:** 23 (27)s, 1m, 10s. **

Work another 22 (30) rows to match back – work 23 (31) rows for right front – mark inner end of 3rd of these rows for 2nd size.
FOR FRONT NECK: Next row: Cast off 4 sts, work to end. Dec 1 st at neck-edge on next 9 (10) rows – 21 (24) sts. Work 3 (2) more rows. Cast off.
RIGHT FRONT: Rejoin yarn to right front sts. Ss 2 rows s. Mark beginning of last row for 1st size. Place dot pattern thus: **1st row:** 10s, 1m, 23 (27)s. Work as left front from ** to end, noting variation.

SLEEVES

With No. 12 (2¾ mm) needles and s cast on 39 (43) sts and work 17 rows in rib as on main part, increasing 4 sts on last row – 43 (47) sts. Change to No. 10 (3¼ mm) needles and work border pattern thus: **1st and 2nd rows:** All s, increasing 1 st each end of 1st row - 45 (49) sts. **3rd row:** Nil (2)s, 1m, [3s, 1m] to last nil (2) sts, nil (2)s. **4th row:** 2 (nil)m, 1s, [3m, 1s] to last 2 (nil) sts, 2 (nil)m. **5th (increase) row:** Inc with m, 3s (inc with s, 1 more s), [1m, 3s] to last 1 (3) st(s), inc with m (1m, 1s, inc with s) – 47 (51) sts. **6th row:** All s. **7th row:** 7 (1)s, [1n, 7s] to last nil (2) sts, nil (1, 1s). **8th to 11th rows:** Keeping continuity of border to match main part, inc 1 st each end of 2nd of these rows – 49 (53) sts. Ss 7 rows s, increasing 1 st each end of 2nd and 6th of these rows – 53 (57) sts.
Place dot pattern thus: **1st row:** 11 (13)s, 1m, 29s, 1m, 11 (13)s. Keeping continuity to

match back, work 1 row, then inc 1 st each end of next row and 4 (5) following 4th rows – 63 (69) sts. Pattern 11 (13) rows. Cast off.

NECKBAND

Join shoulder seams. With right side facing, using No. 12 (2¾ mm) needles and s, pick up and k16 sts up right front neck, k33 (35) back neck sts, then pick up and k 16 sts down left front neck – 65 (67) sts. Beginning with 2nd row, work 9 rows in rib as on main part. Cast off in rib.

BUTTONHOLE/BUTTON BORDER

Using No. 12 (2¾ mm) needles and s, pick up and k63 (71) sts up row-ends of right front. Beginning with 2nd row, work 3 rows in rib as on main part. **Buttonhole row:** Rib 4 (5), work 2 tog, yf or yrn, [rib 7 (8), work 2 tog, yf or yrn] 6 times, rib to end. rib 5 rows. Cast off in rib.
BUTTON BORDER: Work as buttonhole border, omitting buttonholes.

TO MAKE UP

Press. Sew cast-off edge of sleeves to row-ends between markers on back and fronts. Join tiny side and sleeve seams. Add buttons.

HAT

With No. 12 (2¾ mm) needles and s cast on 83 sts and work 16 rows in rib as on cardigan. **Increase row:** Inc, inc, [rib 1, inc, inc] to end – 139 sts. Change to No. 10 (3¼ mm) needles and work 1st to 6th rows of cardigan border pattern. **7th row:** 1s, 1n, [7s, 1n] to last st, 1s. **8th to 11th row:** Keep continuity of pattern to

match cardigan. Ss 5 rows s. Place dot pattern thus: **1st row:** 9s, 1m, [29s, 1m] to last 9 sts, 9s. Work 15 rows to match cardigan, decreasing 1 st at end of last row – 138 sts. **17th (Dec) row:** With s, [k5, k2tog] to last 5 sts, k5 – 119 sts. **18th to 23rd rows:** Keep continuity of dot pattern. Continue in s only. **24th row:** All s. **25 (Dec) row** K1, k3tog, [k3, k3tog] to last st, k1 – 79 sts. **26th row:** P1, [p3tog, p3] to end – 53 sts. **27th row:** K3, k2tog, [k3, k3tog] to end – 36 sts. **28th row:** [P3tog] to end – 12 sts. Break yarn leaving an end, thread through remaining sts, draw up and secure.

TO COMPLETE: Press. Join back seam. Make a pom-pom and sew to top.

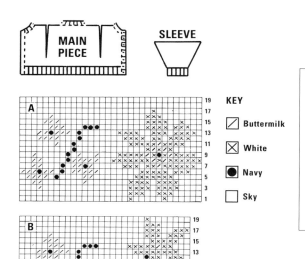

Bobble Top

HE'S A SMART LAD IN THIS FUN-TEXTURED JERSEY

MEASUREMENTS To fit loosely chest sizes 61 (66) (71) cm/24 (26) (28) in.

Actual measurement 79 (83.5) (87.5) cm/31 (32¾) (34½) in. **Side seam** 21 (23) (24.5) cm/8¼ (9) (9½) in.

Length 41 (43.5) (46) cm/16 (17) (18) in. **Sleeve seam** 35 (35.5) (36.5) cm/13¾ (14) (14½) in.

MATERIALS
4 (4) (5) 100 g balls of Sirdar Country Style Aran; No. 6 (5 mm) and No. 8 (4 mm) knitting needles. Yarn used: Cream (411). For stockists, write to Sirdar plc, Flanshaw Lane, Alverthorpe, Wakefield, West Yorkshire WF2 9ND.

TENSION
18 stitches and 25 rows, to 10 x 10 cm/ 4 x 4 in, over pattern, using No. 6 (5 mm) needles.

NOTE
Instructions are given for 61 cm/24 in size. Where they vary, work figures in round brackets for larger sizes. Work instructions in square brackets as stated after 2nd bracket.

This attractive junior sweater has dropped shoulders and a round neck. The pattern is in easy stocking stitch with bobbles, textured diamonds and ridges. The yarn is machine-washable, acrylic/nylon/wool Aran weight.

BACK

With No. 8 (4 mm) needles cast on 61 (65) (69) sts and beginning odd-numbered rows with k1 and even-numbered rows with p1, work 15 rows in single rib. **Increase row:** Rib 4 (6) (8), up1, [rib 6, up1] to last 3 (5) (7) sts, rib to end – 71 (75) (79) sts.
Change to No. 6 (5 mm) needles and ss 6 (10) (14) rows. Place motifs and bobbles thus:
1st row: K24 (26) (28), for chart B, p1, k35, for chart A, p1, k10 (12) (14). This row places motifs. Pattern 11 rows of chart B, also completing chart A. **13th row:** K20 (22) (24), for chart B, p9, k21, for chart B, p1, k to end. Work 5 rows of second chart B, also completing first chart B. **19th row:** K10 (12) (14), for chart A, p1, k37, for chart B, p5, k to end. Work 10 rows, completing charts A and B. **30th row:** P35 (37) (39), k36 (38) (40). **31st row:** All k. **32nd row:** As 30th row. Mark each end of last row for side seams. Ss 2 rows. **35th row:** K nil (2) (4), [mb, k9] 3 times, mb, k to end. **36th row:** All p. 37th row: K5 (7) (9), [mb, k9] 3 times, mb, k to end. Beginning with a p row, ss 2 rows. **40th to 44th rows:** K 4 rows, then p 1 row. **45th row:** K35 (37) (39), [mb, k9] 3 times, mb, k to end. **46th row:** All p. **47th row:** K40 (42) (44), [mb, k9] 3 times, mb, k to end. 48th row: All p. 49th row: K14 (16) (18), for chart B, p1, k to end. **50th row:** K36 (38) (40), p19, for chart B, k3, p to end. **51st row:** K12 (14) (16), for chart B, p5, k to end. **52nd row:** K36 (38) (40), p17, for chart B, k7, p to end. Keeping chart B correct, pattern 2 rows.

55th row: K12 (14) (16) for chart B, p5, k29, for chart A, p1, k to end. Work 5 rows of chart, B and A. **61st row:** Pattern 59 (61) (63), for second chart B, p1, k to end. Work 9 rows of second chart B, at the same time, work remaining 2 rows of chart A and work 4 rows of first chart B. **71st row:** K10 (12) (14), for chart A, p1, pattern to end. Work remaining 8 rows of chart A, at same time, work remaining 6 rows of chart B. Ss 3 (5) (7) rows. Cast off. Place markers 23 (24) (25) sts from each end.

FRONT

Work as back to markers. Pattern another 33 (35) (37) rows.
DIVIDE FOR FRONT NECK: Next row: Pattern 29 (30) (31), and leave these sts on a spare needle for right front neck, pattern next 13 (15) (17) and leave these sts on a st holder, pattern to end and work on these 29 (30) (31) sts for left front neck.
LEFT FRONT NECK: Dec 1 st at neck edge on next row and 5 following alternate rows – 23 (24) (25) sts. Pattern 5 rows. Cast off.
RIGHT FRONT NECK: With right side facing, rejoin yarn to inner end of sts on spare needle and work as left front neck to end.

SLEEVES

With No. 8 (4 mm) needles cast on 35 (37) (39) sts. Rib 19 rows as on back.
Increase row: Rib 4 (5) (3), up1, [rib 4 (3) (3), up1] to last 3 (5) (3) sts, rib to end - 43 (47) (51) sts.
Change to No 6 (5 mm) needles. Ss 2 rows. Place motifs and bobbles thus: **1st row:** K7 (9) (11), for chart A, p1, k35 37 (39). Work 3 rows of chart A, increasing 1 st each end of 2nd of these rows. **5th row:** K4 (6) (8), for first chart A, p9, k19, for second chart A, p1, k to end.

Work 8 rows, completing first and second charts A, and increasing each end of 3rd and 8th of these rows. **14th to 18th rows:** Ss 5 rows, increasing each end of last of these rows. 19th row: K36 (38) (40), for chart B, p1, k to end. Work 5 rows of chart B, increasing each end of 4th of these rows. 25th row: K18 (20) (22), for chart A, p1, pattern to end. Work 10 rows, completing charts A and B, and increasing each end of 3rd and 8th of these rows, then ss 4 rows, increasing each end of 3rd of these rows. **40th row:** P29 (31) (33), k30 (32) (34). **41st row:** All k. **42nd row:** As 40th row. Ss 2 rows, increasing each end of 1st of these rows. **45th row:** K5 (7) (9), [mb, k9] twice, mb, k to end. **46th row:** All p. **47th row:** K nil (2) (4), [mb, k9] 3 times, mb, k to end. **48th (inc) row:** Inc, p to last st, inc. **49th to 54th rows:** K 5 rows, then p 1 row, increasing 1 st at each end of the 5th of these rows. **55th row:** K32 (34) (36), [mb, k9] 3 times, mb, k to end. **56th row:** All p. **57th row:** K16 (18) (20), for chart B, p1, k20, [mb, k9] twice, mb, k to end. **58th (inc) row:** Inc, pattern to last st, inc. **59th row:** K15 (17) (19), for chart B, p5, k to end. **60th row:** K34 (36) (38), pattern to end. **61st row:** K13 (15) (17), for chart B, p9, k to end. **62nd row:** As 60th row. **63rd (inc) row:** Inc, pattern to last st, inc. **64th row:** P49 (51) (53), for chart B, k3, p to end. **65th row:** Pattern 51 (53) (55), for chart A, p1, k to end. Work 8 rows, completing charts A and B, increasing each end of 3rd and 8th (3rd) (nil) of these rows – 73 (75) (77) sts. Ss 1 (3) (5) row(s). Cast off.

NECKBAND

Join right shoulder seam. With right side facing and using No. 8 (4 mm) needles, pick up and k16 sts down left front neck, k13 (15) (17) sts at centre front, pick up and k16 sts up right front neck and 26 (28) (30) sts across centre back neck – 71 (75) (79) sts. K 1 row, then rib 15 rows as on back. Cast off in rib.

TO MAKE UP

Press as given on ball band. Join left shoulder seam, including neckband. Sew cast-off edge of sleeves between markers on back and front. Join sleeve and side seams. Fold neckband in half to wrong side and sl st down. Turn back cuffs.

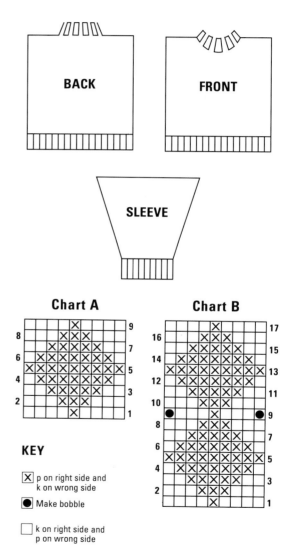

Chart A

Chart B

KEY

☒ p on right side and k on wrong side

● Make bobble

☐ k on right side and p on wrong side

HOWDY
COWBOY

RIDE OUT WILD-WEST STYLE IN THIS BEAUTIFULLY DESIGNED JACKET

MEASUREMENTS To fit sizes 61 (66) cm/24 (26) in.

Actual measurement 67.5 (73) cm/26½ (28¾) in. **Side seam** 16.5 (17.5) cm/6½ (6¾) in.

Length 29.5 (32) cm/11½ (12½) in. **Sleeve seam** 21 (24) cm/8½(9½) in.

MATERIALS

3 (4) 50 g balls of Hayfield Grampian D.K. in main (Millstone 085) and 1 each in red (Claret 020), brown (Nutshell 081) and blue (Bluebell 014); No. 8 (4 mm) and No. 10 (3¼mm) needles; 4 buttons.
Key: main =m, red =r, brown =br, blue =bl.
For stockists, write to Hayfield Textiles Ltd, Glusburn, Keighley, West Yorkshire BD20 8QP.

TENSION

23 stitches and 29 rows, to 10 x 10 cm/4 x 4 in, over stocking stitch, using No. 8 (4 mm) needles.

NOTE

Instructions are given for 61 cm /24 in size. Work figures in round brackets for larger size. Instructions in square brackets are worked as stated after 2nd bracket.

This jacket has dropped shoulders, and buttons to a cosy shawl collar. It is knitted mainly in stocking stitch. The yarn is machine-washable .

BACK

With No. 10 (3¼ mm) needles and m cast on 76 (82) sts and single rib 14 rows, increasing 1 st at end of last row — 77 (83) sts. Change to No. 8 (4 mm) needles and k 1 row. Work pattern band, which is entirely in ss, beginning with a p row, so only colour details are given. When changing colours, wind yarn round one just used, to avoid leaving a gap. **1st row:** All r. **2nd and 3rd rows:** All m. **4th row:** Nil (1r, 1m, 1br), [* 2m, 1bl, 2m, 2r, 1m, 1br, 1m, 2r, 2m, 1bl, 2m *, 1br, 1m, 2r, 2m, 1bl, 2m, 2r, 1m, 1br] twice, then * to * again, nil (1br, 1m, 1r). **5th row:** 1m (1m, 1br, 2m), [* 3bl, 1m, 1r, 1m, 1br, 1bl, 1br, 1m, 1r, 1m, 3bl *, 2m, 1br, 1m, 1r, 1m, 3bl, 1m, 1r, 1m, 1br, 2m] twice, then * to * again, 1m (2m, 1br, 1m). **6th row:** Nil (1br, 2m), [* 2bl, 1r, 2bl, 1m, 1br, 1bl, 1r, 1bl, 1br, 1m, 2bl, 1r, 2bl *, 2m, 1br, 1m, 2bl, 1r, 2bl, 1m, 1br, 2m] twice, then * to * again, nil (2m, 1br). **7th to 11th rows:** Work 5th row back to 1st row, in that reverse order. With m only, ss 20 (24) rows. Place eagle motif thus: **1st row:** 37 (40) m, 2br, 38 (41) m. Reading even-numbered rows from left to right and odd-numbered rows from right to left, work 3 rows of chart. Mark each end of last row for side seams. Work remaining 19 rows of chart. With m only, ss 17 (21) rows.
FOR SHOULDERS: Cast off 22 (24) sts at start of next 2 rows. Leave 33 (35) sts on a needle.

FRONT

LEFT FRONT: With No. 10 (3¼ mm) needles and m cast on 36 (40) sts and single rib 14 rows,

increasing 1 (nil) st at end of last row — 37 (40) sts. Change to No. 8 (4 mm) needles and k 1 row. Place pattern band thus: **1st row:** All r. **2nd and 3rd rows:** All m. ** **4th row:** Nil (1r, 1m, 1br), 2m, 1bl, 2m, 2r, 1m, 1br, 1m, 2r, 2m, 1bl, 2m, 1br, 1m, 2r, 2m, 1bl, 2m, 2r, 1m, 1br, 2m, 1bl, 2m, 2r. **5th row:** 1m, 1r, 1m, 3bl, 2m, 1br, 1m, 1r, 1m, 3bl, 1m, 1r, 1m, 1br, 2m, 3bl, 1m, 1r, 1m, 1br, 1bl, 1br, 1m, 1r, 1m, 3bl, then 1m (2m, 1br, 1m). Pattern a further 6 rows to match back. With m only, ss 8 (12) rows. Place bow and arrow motif thus: **1st row:** 14 (17) m, 1r, 7m, 1bl, 14m.
*** Reading rows as on back, work 14 rows following chart.
TO SHAPE FRONT EDGE: Completing chart, then working in m only, dec 1 st at beginning — read end here when working right front — of next row and 14 (15) following alternate rows, marking side edge of 1st of these rows for side seam — 22 (24) sts. Ss 8 (10) rows — ss 9 (11) rows here when working right front. Cast off for shoulder.
RIGHT FRONT: Work as left front to **. **4th row:** 2r, 2m, 1bl, 2m, 1br, 1m, 2r, 2m, 1bl, 2m, 2r, 1m, 1br, 2m, 1bl, 2m, 2r, 1m, 1br, 1m, 2r, 2m, 1bl, 2m, then nil (1br, 1m, 1r). **5th row:** 1m (1m, 1br, 2m), 3bl, 1m, 1r, 1m, 1br, 1bl, 1br, 1m, 1r, 1m, 3bl, 2m, 1br, 1m, 1r, 1m, 3bl, 1m, 1r, 1m, 1br, 2m, 3bl, 1m, 1r, 1m. Pattern a further 6 rows to match back. With m only, ss 8 (12) rows. Place wigwam motif thus: **1st row:** 7m, 7br, 5r, 7br, 11 (14) m. Work as left front from *** to end, noting variation.

SLEEVES

With No. 10 (3¼ mm) needles and m cast on 44 (46) sts and work 14 rows in single rib, increasing 3 (1) st(s) across last row — 47 sts. Change to No. 8 (4 mm) needles and k 1 row. Place pattern band thus: **1st row:** All r.
2nd and 3rd rows: All m. **4th row:** * 2m, 1br,

1m, 2r, 2m, 1bl, 2m, 2r, 1m, 1br, 2m *, 1bl, 2m, 2r, 1m, 1br, 1m, 2r, 2m, 1bl, work from * to *. **5th row:** 1bl, * 2m, 1br, 1m, 1r, 1m, 3bl, 1m, 1r, 1m, 1br, 2m *, 3bl, 1m, 1r, 1m, 1br, 1bl, 1br, 1m, 1r, 1m, 3bl, work from * to *, 1bl. Keeping continuity of pattern band to match back, and then working in m only, work 2 rows, then inc 1 st each end of next row and the 4 (7) following 6th rows — 57 (63) sts. Ss 17 (7) rows. Cast off.

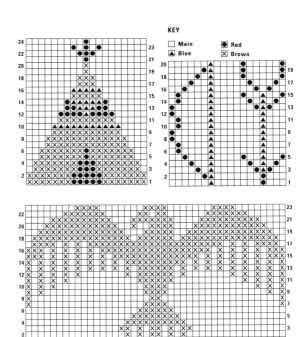

FRONT BAND AND COLLAR

Join shoulder seams. With right side facing, rejoin br and using No. 10 (3¼ mm) needles, pick up and k50 (53) sts from straight row-ends of right front to 1st front dec, 44 (47) sts to shoulder, work across back neck sts thus: K3 (4), up1, k2, up1, [k3, up1, k2, up1] 5 times, k3 (4), then pick up and k44 (47) sts down left front to 1st front dec, then 50 (53) sts from straight row-ends to cast-on edge — 233 (247) sts. **1st rib row:** P1, [k1, p1] to end.
TO SHAPE FOR COLLAR: 1st row: Rib 147 (154), turn. **2nd row:** Rib 61, turn. **3rd row:** Rib 65, turn. **4th row:** Rib 69, turn. Continue in this way for a further 16 (18) turning rows, taking in an extra 4 sts, as before, on each row. **Next row:** Rib to end of row. Rib another 2 rows across all sts. **1st buttonhole row:** Rib 183 (194), cast off 2, [rib a further 12 (13) sts, cast off 2] 3 times, rib remaining 2 sts. **2nd buttonhole row:** Rib to end, casting on 2 sts over each group cast-off in previous row. Rib 2 rows. Cast off in rib.

TO MAKE UP

Press as given on ball band. Sew cast-off edge of sleeves to row-ends between markers on back and fronts. Join side and sleeve seams. Add buttons. Roll collar to right side.

KEY
□ Main   ● Red
▲ Blue   ⊠ Brown

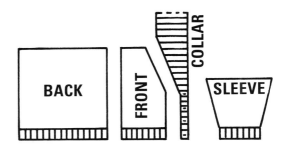

BACK   FRONT   COLLAR   SLEEVE

THE BRIGHT SIDE

SHE'S A LITTLE RAY OF SUNSHINE IN THIS BRIGHTLY COLOURED SWEATER

MEASUREMENTS To fit sizes 56 (61) (66) cm/22 (24) (26) in.

Actual measurement 67.5 (72.5) (77.5) cm/26½ (28½) (30½) in. **Side seam** 19 (20) (21.5) cm/7½ (7¾) (8½) in.

Length 32 (35) (37.5) cm/12½ (13¾) (14¾) in. **Sleeve seam** 26 (28) (30) cm/10¼ (11) (11¾) in.

MATERIALS

5 (6) (7) 50 g balls of Hayfield Silky Cotton D.K. in yellow (Aztec 025), and 1 (1) (2) balls each in red (Eldorado 027) and blue (Regatta 031); No. 8 (4 mm) and No. 10 (3¼ mm) knitting needles. Key yellow = y, red = r, blue = bl, For stockists, write to Hayfield Textiles Ltd, Glusburn, Keighley, West Yorkshire BD20 8QP.

TENSION

24 stitches and 30 rows, to 10 x 10 cm/4 x 4 in, over pattern, using No. 8 (4 mm) needles.

NOTE

Instructions are given for 56 cm/22 in size. Where they vary, work figures in round brackets for larger sizes. Work instructions in square brackets as stated after 2nd bracket.

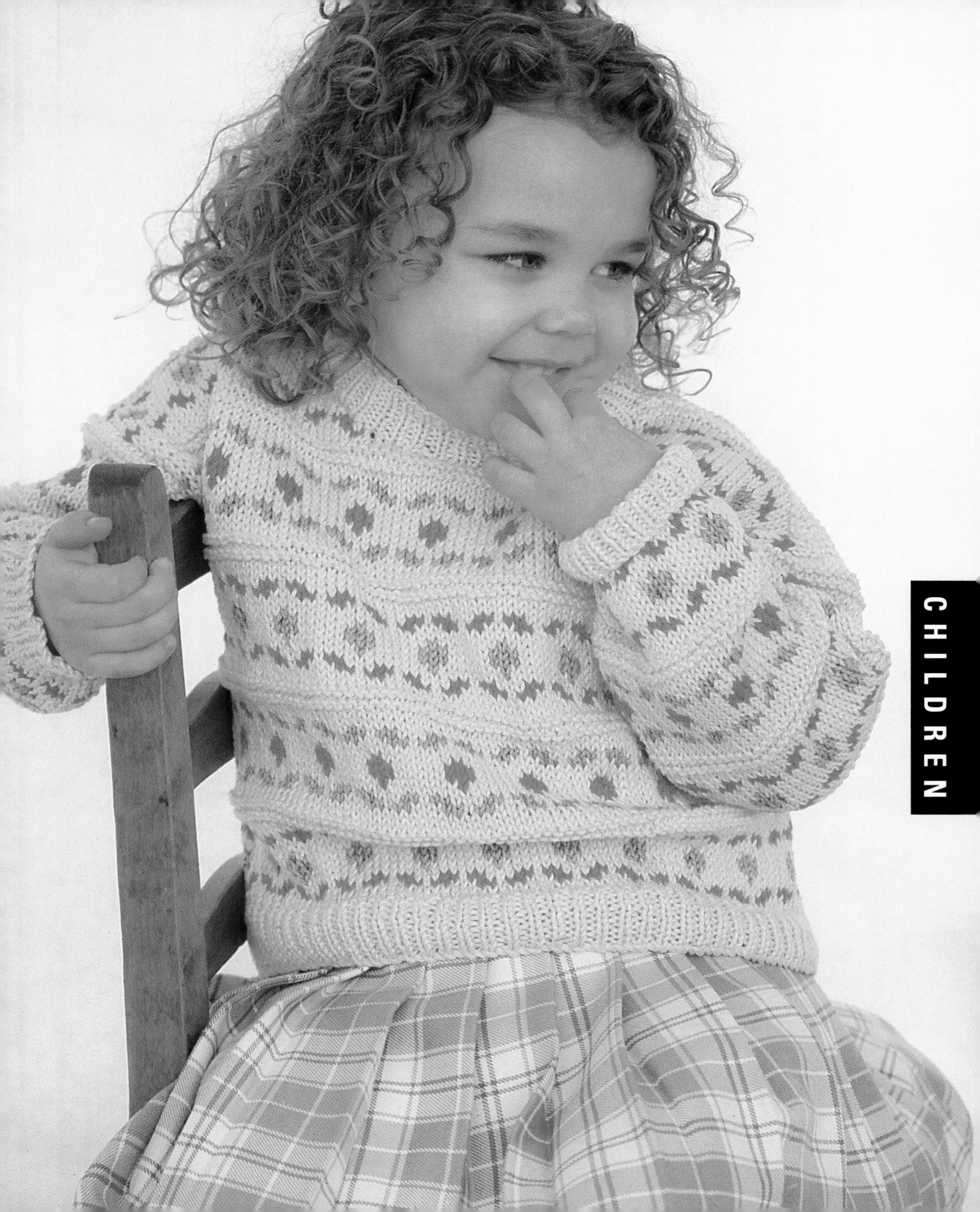

The easy contrast patterning in this sunny sweater is worked in stocking-stitch bands, separated by garter-stitch ridges. It has dropped shoulders and a round neck. The yarn is machine-washable, mercerised pure cotton D.K., which has a silky finish.

BACK

With No. 10 (3¼ mm) needles and y cast on 74 (80) (86) sts and single rib 9 rows.
Increase row: Rib 4 (7) (10), inc, [rib 10, inc] to last 3 (6) (9) sts, rib to end - 81 (87) (93) sts.
Change to No. 8 (4 mm) needles and joining in and breaking off colours as required, work the 36-row pattern, which is worked entirely in ss beginning with a k row, so only the colour details are given. Avoid drawing yarn too tightly across back of work and when changing from one colour to another, wind yarn round the one just used, to avoid leaving a gap.
1st and 2nd rows: All y. **3rd row:** 1y, 2r (1y, 2r, 1y, 2r) (1r), [3y, 2r, 1y, 2r] to last 6 (1) (4) st(s), 3y, 2 r, 1y (1y) (3y, 1r). **4th row:** 2y (2r, 3y) (nil), [2r, 1y, 2r, 3y] to last 7 (2) (5) sts, 2r, 1y, 2r, 2y (2r) (2r, 1y, 2r). **5th row:** All y. **6th row:** Nil (3) (6) y, [1bl, 7y] to last 1 (4) (7) st(s), 1bl, then nil (3) (6) y. **7th and 8th rows:** 2bl (2y, 3bl) (nil), [5y, 3bl] to last 7 (2) (5) sts, 5y, 2bl (2y) (5y). **9th to 14th rows:** As 6th row back to 1st row, in that reverse order. **15th to 18th rows:** With y, k 4 rows. **19th to 36th rows:** As 1st to 18th rows, but using r instead of bl and bl instead of r. Pattern a further 10 (14) (18) rows. Mark each end of last row for side seams. Pattern a further 38 (42) (46) rows.
FOR SHOULDERS: Cast off 25 (27) (29) sts at beginning of next 2 rows. Leave remaining 31 (33) (35) sts on a spare needle.

FRONT

Work as back to markers. Pattern another 19 (23) (27) rows.
DIVIDE FOR FRONT NECK: Next row: Pattern 35 (37) (39) and leave these sts on a spare needle for right front neck, pattern the next 11 (13) (15) sts and leave them on a st holder, pattern to end and work on these 35 (37) (39) sts for left front neck.
LEFT FRONT NECK: Pattern 1 row. Cast off 2 sts at beginning of next row and 2 following alternate rows, then dec 1 st at neck edge on next row and 3 following alternate rows – 25 (27) (29) sts.
Pattern 5 rows. Cast off for shoulder.
RIGHT FRONT NECK: With right side facing, rejoin appropriate yarn to inner end of sts on spare needle.
Cast off 2 sts at beginning of next row and 2 following alternate rows, pattern 1 row, then dec 1 st at neck edge on next row and 3 following alternate rows – 25 (27) (29) sts.
Pattern 6 rows. Cast off for shoulder.

SLEEVES

With No. 10 (3¼ mm) needles and y cast on 40 (46) (52) sts and single rib 10 rows, increasing 3 sts evenly across last row – 43 (49) (55) sts.
Change to No. 8 (4 mm) needles and place pattern thus: **1st and 2nd rows:** All y. **3rd row:** Nil (1y, 2r) (1y, 2r, 1y, 2r), [3y, 2r, 1y, 2r] to last 3 (6) (1) st(s), 3y (3y, 2r, 1y) (1y). **4th row:** 1r, 1y, 2r (2y, 2r, 1y, 2r) (2r), [3y, 2r, 1y, 2r] to last 7 (2) (5) sts, 3y, 2r, 1y, 1r (2y) (3y, 2r). Keeping continuity of pattern to match back, and taking extra sts into pattern as they occur, inc 1 st at each end of next row and 8 following 6th (8th) (8th) rows – 61 (67) (73) sts. Pattern 15 (5) (11) rows. Cast off.

NECKBAND

Join right shoulder seam. With right side facing and using No. 10 (3¼ mm) needles and y, pick up and k18 sts down left front neck, k across 11 (13) (15) sts at centre front, pick up and k18 sts up right front neck, then k across 31 (33) (35) sts at back neck — 78 (82) (86) sts.
Single rib 8 rows. Cast off in rib.

TO MAKE UP

Press as given on ball band. Join left shoulder seam, including neckband. Sew cast-off edge of sleeves between markers on back and front. Join sleeve and side seams.

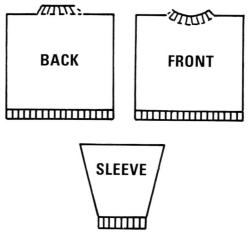

BACK

FRONT

SLEEVE

BUTTONS

AND

BOWS

———

SHE LOOKS BONNY IN THIS TARTAN-TRIM CARDIGAN

MEASUREMENTS To fit loosely sizes 56 (61-66) (71-76) cm/22 (24-26) (28-30) in.

Actual measurement 68 (81.5) (93) cm/26¾ (32¼) (36½) in. **Side seam** 22 (25) (26.5) cm/8½ (9¾) (10½) in.

Length 36.5 (40) (42) cm/14½ (15¾) (16½) in. **Sleeve seam** 19 (21) (27) cm/7½ (8¼) (10½) in.

MATERIALS

6 (6) (7) 50 g balls of Hayfield Traditional Pure Wool D.K.; No. 8 (4 mm) and No. 10 (3¼ mm) knitting needles; a cable needle; 3 metres/3⅜ yards tartan ribbon; 7 buttons. Yarn used: Morello (002).
For stockists, write to Hayfield Textiles Ltd, Glusburn, Keighley, West Yorkshire BD20 8QP. Tel: 0535 633333.

TENSION

27 stitches and 30 rows to 10 x 10 cm/4 x 4 in, over pattern, and 32 rows to 10 cm/4 in in depth, over stocking stitch, using No. 8 (4 mm) needles.

NOTE

Instructions are given for 56 cm size. Where they vary, work figures in round for larger sizes. Work instructions in square brackets as stated after 2nd bracket.

A pretty cardigan knitted in cable and moss stitch diamond panels with stocking-stitch yoke, trimmed with tartan bows. It has dropped shoulders, and buttons to a round neck. The yarn is machine-washable, pure wool D.K.

BACK

With No. 10 (3¼ mm) needles cast on 67 (79) (89) sts and, beginning odd-numberd rows with k1 and even-numbered rows with p1, work 11 (11) (15) rows in single rib. **Increase row:** Rib 9 (10) (8), up1, [rib 2, up1] to last 8 (9) (7) sts, rib to end – 93 (110) (127) sts.
Change to No. 8 (4 mm) needles. 1st pattern row: P2, k4, p2, [k9, p2, k4, p2] to end. **2nd row:** K2, p4, k2, [p9, k2, p4, k2] to end. **3rd row:** P2, c4, p2, [k4, p1, k4, p2, c4, p2] to end. **4th row:** K2, p4, k2, [p3, k1, p1, k1, p3, k2, p4, k2] to end. **5th row:** P2, k4, p2, [k2, p1, k1, p1, k1, p1, k2, p2, k4, p2] to end. **6th row:** K2, p4, k2, [p1, k1, p1, k1, p1, k1, p1, k1, p1, k2, p4, k2] to end. These 6 rows form 8-st cable panel. Keeping cable panel correct, continue thus: **7th row:** Pattern 8, [k2, p1, k1, p1, k1, p1, k2, pattern 8] to end. **8th row:** Pattern 8, [p3, k1, p1, k1, p3, pattern 8] to end. **9th row:** Pattern 8, [k4, p1, k4, pattern 8] to end. **10th row:** Pattern 8, [p9, pattern 8] to end. These 10 rows form the diamond panel. Keeping continuity of all panels, pattern another 46 (54) (56) rows. Mark each end for side seam. Pattern 14 (16) (14) rows.
Decrease row: K6, p2tog, k9, p2tog, [k4, p2tog, k9 p2tog] to last 6 sts, k6 – 83 (98) (113) sts.
Beginning with a P row, ss 25 (27) (31) rows.
FOR SHOULDERS: Cast off 15 (18) (21) sts at beginning of next 4 rows.
Leave 23 (26) (29) sts on a spare needle.

LEFT FRONT

With No. 10 (3¼ mm) needles cast on 29 (35) (41) sts and rib 11 (11) (15) rows as on back. **Increase row:** Rib 3 (2) (4), up1, [rib 2, up1] to last 2 (1) (3) st(s), rib to end – 42 (52) (59) sts.
Change to No. 8 (4 mm) needles.
1st pattern row: [P2, k4, p2, k9] to last 8 (1) (8) st(s), p2, k4, p2 (p1) (p2, k4, p2). **2nd row:** K2, p4, k2 (k1) (k2, p4, k2), [k9, k2, p4, k2] to end. These 2 rows set position of pattern. Keeping pattern correct to match back, work another 54 (62) (64) rows. Mark end of last row for side seam. Pattern 14 (16) (14) rows. **Decrease row:** K6, [p2tog, k9, p2tog, k4] to last 2 (12) (2) sts, k2 more (p2tog, k10) (k2 more) – 38 (47) (53) sts. Beginning with a p row, ss 12 (12) (14) rows.
** FOR NECK: Cast off 3 (4) (4) sts at beginning of next row and 2 sts on the following alternate row. Dec 1 st at neck edge on next 3 (5) (5) rows – 30 (36) (42) sts. Ss 7 (7) (9) rows.
FOR SHOULDER: Cast off 15 (18) (21) sts at beginning of next row. Work 1 row. Cast off 15 (18) (21) sts.

RIGHT FRONT

With No. 10 (3¼ mm) needles cast on 29 (35) (41) sts and rib 11 (11) (15) rows as on back. Change to No. 8 (4 mm) needles. **1st pattern row:** P2, k4, p2 (p1) (p2, k4, p2), [k9, p2, k4, p2] to end. **2nd row:** [K2, p4, k2, p9] to last 8 (1) (8) st(s), k2, p4, k2 (k1) (k2, p4, k2). These 2 rows set position of pattern. Keeping pattern correct to match back, work another 54 (62) (64) rows. Mark beginning of last row for side seam. Pattern 14 (16) (14) rows. **Decrease row:** K6 (k10, p2tog, k4) (k6), [p2tog, k9, p2tog, k4] to last 2 sts, k2 more – 38 (47) (53) sts. Ss 13 (13) (15) rows. Work as left front from ** to end.

SLEEVES

With No. 10 (3¼ mm) needles cast on 35 (37) (39) sts and rib 11 (11) (15) rows as on back. **Increase row:** Rib 4 (3) (2), [up1, rib 1, up1, rib 2] to last st, rib 1 – 55 (59) (63) sts. Change to No. 8 (4 mm) needles.
1st pattern row: Nil (p2) (k2, p2), k4, [p2, k9, p2, k4] to last nil (2) (4) sts, nil (p2) (p2, k2).
2nd row: Nil (k2) (p2, k2), p4, [k2, p9, k2, p4] to last nil (2) (4) sts, nil (k2) (k2, p2).
These 2 rows set position of pattern. Keeping pattern correct to match back, inc 1 st each end of next row and 7 (8) (9) following 6th rows – 71 (77) (83) sts. Pattern 1 (1) (9) row(s). Cast off.

NECKBAND

Join shoulder seams. With right side facing, using No. 10 (3¼ mm) needles, pick up and k18 (20) (22) sts from right front neck, k back neck sts, increasing 2 (1) (nil), then pick up and k18 (20) (22) sts from left front neck – 61 (67) (73) sts.
Beginning with an even-numbered row, rib 7 (7) (9) rows as on back. Cast off in rib.

BUTTONHOLE BAND

With right side facing, using No. 10 (3¼ mm) needles, pick up and k91 (97) (103) sts from row-ends of right front edge, including neckband.
Beginning with an even-numbered row, rib 3 rows as on back. **1st buttonhole row:** Rib 3, cast off 2, [rib a further 11 (12) (13) sts, cast off 2] 6 times, rib to end. **2nd buttonhole row:** Rib to end, casting on 2 sts over each group cast off in previous row.
Rib 2 rows. Cast off in rib.

BUTTON BAND

Work as for buttonhole band, omitting buttonholes.

TO MAKE UP

Press as given on ball band. Sew cast-off edge of sleeves to row-ends between markers on back and front. Join side and sleeve seams. Add buttons. Make and add a ribbon bow at top of each diamond panel on back and front.

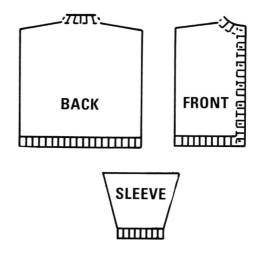

CHILDREN

COAT OF MANY COLOURS

PRETTY AS A PICTURE IN A COLOURFUL TUNIC-STYLE SWEATER

MEASUREMENTS To fit sizes 66 (71) (76) (81) (86) (91) (97) (102) (107) (112) cm/26 (28) (30) (32) (34) (36) (38) (40) (42) (44) in.

Actual measurement 79 (85.5) (92) (99) (105.5) (112) (116.5) (123.5) (130) (134.5) cm/31 (33¾) (36¼) (39) (41½) (45¾) (45¾) (48¾) (51¼) (53) in.

Side seam 31.5 (34) (36.5) (42) (42) (42) (42) (42) (42) (42) cm/12½ (13½) (14½) (16½) (16½) (16½) (16½) (16½) (16½) (16½) in.

Length 50.5 (54.5) (59) (67) (67.5) (68.5) (69.5) (70) (71) (72) cm/19¾ (21½) (23¼) (26½) (26¾) (27) (27¼) (27½) (28) (28½) in.

Sleeve seam 35 (37) (38.5) (44.5) (44.5) (44.5) (44.5) (44.5) (44.5) (44.5) cm/13¾ (14½) (15) (17½) (17½) (17½) (17½) (17½) (17½) (17½) in.

MATERIALS

4 (4) (5) (5) (6) (7) (7) (8) (8) (9) 100 g balls of Chevy Premier Aran; No. 7 (4½ mm) and No. 9 (3¾ mm) knitting needles.
Yarn used Carousel (4818).
For stockists, write to Tootal Craft, Units 1/2 Westpoint Enterprise Park, Clarence Avenue, Trafford Park, Manchester M17 1QS.

TENSION

18 stitches and 24 rows, to 10 x 10 cm, over stocking stitch, using No. 7 (4½ mm) knitting needles.

NOTE

Instructions are given for 66 cm/26 in size. Where they vary, work figures in round brackets for larger sizes. Work instructions in square brackets as stated after the 2nd bracket.

SPECIAL NOTE

It is advisable first to go through the instructions and underline in red all the figures relating to the size to be worked.

These matching tunic-style sweaters have dropped shoulders, a round neck, and side slits. They are knitted mainly in stocking stitch with moss-stitch welts and double rib cuffs. The double rib neckband is finished with a stocking stitch edging that rolls over. The yarn is machine-washable, acrylic Aran weight, which comes in plain colours or the bright print used here.

BACK

With No. 9 (3¾ mm) needles cast on 71 (77) (83) (89) (95) (101) (105) (111) (117) (121) sts and work in mst st as follows:
Mst row: K1, [p1, k1] to end.
Mst a further 7 (7) (7) (9) (9) (9) (9) (9) (9) (9) rows.
Change to No. 7 (4½ mm) needles and, beginning with a k row, ss 68 (74) (80) (92) (92) (92) (92) (92) (92) (92) rows. Mark each end of the last, row, to denote end of side seams.
Beginning with a k row, ss a further 44 (48) (52) (58) (60) (62) (64) (66) (68) (70) rows.
FOR SHOULDERS: Cast off 23 (25) (27) (29) (31) (33) (35) (37) (39) (41) sts at the beginning of each of the next 2 rows. Leaving remaining 25 (27) (29) (31) (33) (35) (35) (37) (39) (39) sts on a spare needle.

FRONT

With No. 9 (3¾ mm) needles cast on 71 (77) (83) (89) (95) (101) (105) (111) (117) (121) sts and work in mst as follows:
Mst row: K1, [p1, k1] to end. Mst a further 7 (7) (7) (9) (9) (9) (9) (9) (9) (9) rows.
Change to No. 7 (4½ mm) needles and, beginning with a k row, ss 68 (74) (80) (92) (92) (92) (92) (92) (92) (92) rows. Mark

each end of the last row, to denote end of side seams. Beginning with a k row, ss a further 25 (29) (33) (37) (39) (41) (43) (45) (47) (49) rows.
DIVIDE STS FOR FRONT NECK: Next row: P29 (31) (33) (36) (38) (41) (43) (45) (48) (49) and leave these sts on a spare needle for right front neck, p the next 13 (15) (17) (17) (19) (19) (19) (21) (21) (21) sts and leave them on a st holder for collar, p to end and work on remaining 29 (31) (33) (36) (38) (41) (43) (45) (48) (50) sts for left front neck.
LEFT FRONT NECK: Dec 1 st at neck edge on each of the next 3 (3) (3) (3) (3) (3) (3) (3) (5) (5) rows and then on the 3 (3) (3) (4) (4) (5) (5) (5) (4) (4) following alternate rows - 23 (25) (27) (29) (31) (33) (35) (37) (39) (41) sts. Beginning with a p row, ss 9 (9) (9) (9) (9) (9) (7) (7) (7) (7) rows.
Cast off for shoulder.
RIGHT FRONT NECK: With right side of work facing, rejoin yarn to inner end of sts on spare needle. Dec 1 st at neck edge on each of the next 3 (3) (3) (3) (3) (3) (3) (3) (5) (5) rows and then on the 3 (3) (3) (4) (4) (5) (5) (5) (4) (4) following alternate rows − 23 (25) (27) (29) (31) (33) (35) (37) (39) (41) sts. Beginning with a p row, ss a further 10 (10) (10) (10) (10) (8) (8) (8) (8) (8) rows. Cast off for shoulder.

SLEEVES

With No. 9 (3¾ mm) needles cast on 38 (42) (42) (46) (46) (46) (50) (50) (54) (58) sts and beginning odd-numbered rows with k2 and even-numbered rows with p2, work 15 (15) (15) (19) (19) (19) (19) (19) (19) rows in double rib. **Increase row:** Rib 5 (3) (3) (5) (5) (5) (4) (4) (6) (4), inc, [rib 3 (4) (4) (4) (4) (4) (5) (5) (5) (6), inc] to last 4 (3) (3) (5) (5) (5) (3) (3) (5) (4) sts, rib to end − 46 (50) (50) (54) (54) (54) (58) (58) (62) (66) sts. Change to No. 7 (4½ mm) needles and, beginning with a k row, ss 4 rows.

Continuing in ss, inc 1 st at each end of the next row and the 9 (10) (13) (16) (17) (18) (18) (19) (19) (19) following 6th (6th) (4th) (4th) (4th) (4th) (4th) (4th) (4th) (4th) rows – 66 (72) (78) (88) (90) (92) (96) (98) (102) (106) sts.

Beginning with a p row, ss a further 11 (9) (21) (19) (15) (11) (11) (7) (7) (7) rows. Cast off.

COLLAR

Join right shoulder seam. With right side of work facing and using No. 9 (3¾ mm) needles, pick up and k19 (19) (19) (21) (21) (21) (21) (21) (21) (21) sts down left front neck, k across the 13 (15) (17) (17) (19) (19) (19) (21) (21) (21) sts at centre front, pick up and k19 (19) (19) (21) (21) (21) (21) (21) (21) (21) sts up right front neck, then k across the 25 (27) (29) (31) (33) (35) (35) (37) (39) (39) sts at back neck, increasing 2 (decreasing 2) (decreasing 2) (nil) (nil) (decreasing 2) (decreasing 2) (decreasing 2) (nil) (nil) sts across these sts - 78 (78) (82) (90) (94) (94) (94) (98) (102) (102) sts. Work 6 rows in rib as given for sleeves. Beginning with a p row, ss 13 (13) (13) (15) (15) (15) (15) (15) (15) (15) rows. Cast off.

TO MAKE UP

Press as given on ball band. Join left shoulder seam, continuing seam across collar. Sew cast-off edge of sleeves to row-ends between markers on back and front. Join sleeve seams. Join side seams, leaving mst borders free to form side vents.

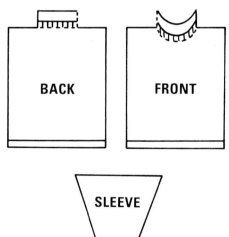

BACK   FRONT

SLEEVE

CHILDREN

BEAUTIFUL
BROWNIE

A PRETTY CARDIGAN WITH A SPECIAL FRILL-EDGED COLLAR

MEASUREMENTS To fit sizes 61 (66) (71) (76) cm/24 (26) (28) (30) in.
Actual measurement 73.5 (78) (82.5) (88) cm/29 (30¾) (32½) (34½) in. **Side seam** 20.5 (22) (24) (26) cm/8 (8½) (9½) (10¼) in.
Length 38 (40.5) (43.5) (46) cm/15 (16) (17) (18) in. **Sleeve seam** 28.5 (33) (38.5) (42.5) cm/11 (13) (15) (16¾) in.

MATERIALS

9 (10) (11) (13) 50 g balls Tivoli Aranmore; No. 6 (5 mm) and No. 8 (4 mm) knitting needles; cable needle; 5 buttons. Yarn used Brown (828).
For stockists, write to Unit 3, New Street Industrial Estate, Bridgetown, Cannock, Staffs WS11 3DD.

TENSION

18 stitches and 30 rows to 10 x 10 cm/4 x 4 in over moss stitch, and the 21-stitch pattern panel to 9 cm/3½ in in width, using No. 6 (5 mm) needles.

NOTE

Instructions are given for 61 cm/24 in size. Work figures in round brackets for larger sizes. Instructions in square brackets are worked as stated after 2nd bracket.

This cosy cardigan has dropped shoulders, and buttons to a shawl collar. It is knitted in crunchy moss stitch, with twist panels down each front, and the moss-stitch collar has a frilled edging sewn on afterwards. The yarn is machine-washable pure wool Aran.

BACK

With No. 6 (5 mm) needles cast on 65 (69) (73) (79) sts, and, beginning odd-numbered rows with k1 and even-numbered rows with p1, work 6 rows single rib. **Mst row:** P1, [k1, p1] to end. Mst another 55 (59) (65) (69) rows. Mark each end of last row for side seams. Mst another 50 (54) (56) (60) rows. **FOR SHOULDERS:** Cast off 21 (23) (24) (26) sts at beginning of next 2 rows. Cast off 23 (23) (25) (27) sts.

LEFT FRONT

With No. 6 (5 mm) needles cast on 37 (39) (41) (43) sts. Single rib 6 rows as back. Work the 20-row pattern panel thus: **1st row:** [P1, k1] 4 (4) (5) (5) times, p nil (1) (nil) (1), for panel p7, c3bp, k1, c3fp, p7, p nil (1), (nil) (1), [k1, p1] 4 (4) (5) (5) times. This row sets mst for 8 (9) (10) (11) sts each side of pattern panel.
2nd row: Mst 8 (9) (10) (11), for panel k7, p3, for mst k1, p3, k7, mst 8 (9) (10) (11).
3rd row: Mst 8 (9) (10) (11), p6, c3b, for mst p1, k1, p1, c3f, p6, mst to end. **4th row:** Mst 8 (9) (10) (11), k6, p2, k1, [p1, k1] twice, p2, k6, mst to end.
These rows set mst between cables. **5th row:** Mst 8 (9) (10) (11), p5, c3bp, mst 5, c3fp, p5, mst to end. **6th row:** Mst 8 (9) (10) (11), k5, p2, mst 7, p2, k5, mst to end. **7th row:** Mst 8 (9) (10) (11), P4, c3b, mst 7, c3f, p4,

mst to end. **8th row:** Mst 8 (9) (10) (11), k4, p2, mst 9, p2, k4, mst to end. **9th row:** Mst 8 (9) (10) (11), P3, c3bp, mst 9, c3fp, p3, mst to end. **10th row:** Mst 8 (9) (10) (11), k3, p2, mst 11, p2, k3, mst to end. **11th row:** Mst 8 (9) (10) (11), p2, c3b, mst 11, c3f, p2, mst to end. **12th row:** Mst 8 (9) (10) (11), k2, p2, mst 13, p2, k2, mst to end. **13th row:** Mst 8 (9) (10) (11), p1, c3bp, mst 13, c3fp, p1, mst to end. **14th row:** Mst 8 (9) (10) (11), k1, p2, mst 15, p2, k1, mst to end. **15th row:** Mst 8 (9) (10) (11), p1, k2, mst 15, k2, p1, mst to end. **16th row:** Mst 8 (9) (10) (11), k1, p2, mst 15, p2, k1, mst to end. **17th row:** Mst 8 (9) (10) (11), p1, c4f, mst 11, c4b, p1, mst to end. **18th row:** Mst 8 (9) (10) (11), k3, p2, mst 11, p2, k3, mst to end. **19th row:** Mst 8 (9) (10) (11), p3, c4f, mst 7, c4b, p3, mst to end. **20th row:** Mst 8 (9) (10) (11), k8, p2, k1, p2, k8, mst to end. Pattern another 36 (40) (46) (50) rows. Mark end – read beginning here for right front – of last row for side seam.
TO SHAPE FRONT EDGE: Continue in pattern and dec 1 st at front edge of next row and 7 (5) (6) (10) following 4th rows, then the 2 (4) (4) (1) following 6th row(s) – 27 (29) (30) (31) sts. Pattern another 9 (9) (7) (13) rows – pattern 10 (10) (8) (14) rows here when working right front. Cast off for shoulder.

RIGHT FRONT

Work as left front, noting variations.

SLEEVES

With No. 8 (4 mm) needles cast on 31 (33) (35) (37) sts and single rib 14 rows as back, increasing 4 sts across last row – 35 (37) (39) (41) sts.
Change to No. 6 (5 mm) needles and mst 2 rows as on back. Inc 1 st each end of next row and the 6 (11) (4) (7) following 6th

CHILDREN

(6th) (8th) (8th) rows, then the 5 (1) (9) (7) following 4th (4th) (6th) (6th) row(s) — 59 (63) (67) (71) sts. Mst another 11 rows. Cast off in mst.

COLLAR

With No. 6 (5 mm) needles cast on 111 (119) (127) (135) sts and mst 2 rows as on back. **3rd row:** K1, [k2tog, pass 1st st over 2nd and off needle] 3 times, mst to end. **4th to 10th rows:** As 3rd row — 63 (71) (79) (87) sts. **11th row:** K1, [k2tog, pass 1st st over 2nd and off needle] twice, mst to end. **12th to 16th rows:** As 11th row. Cast off 39 (47) (55) (63) sts in mst.

COLLAR EDGINGS

LEFT SIDE: With No. 8 (4 mm) needles cast on 179 (189) (199) (209) sts. **1st row (wrong side):** [P7, k3] to last 9 sts, p7, k2. **2nd row:** P2, [skpo, k3, k2tog, p3] to last 7 sts, skpo, k3, k2tog. **3rd and following alternate row:** K and p to end with sts as set. **4th row:** P2, [skpo, k1, k2tog, p3] to last 5 sts, skpo, k1, k2tog. **6th row:** P2, [sl1, k2tog, psso, p3] to last 3 sts, sl1, k2tog, psso. **7th row:** [P1, k3] to last 3 sts, p1, k2 — 71 (75) (79) (83) sts. Cast off with sts as set.
RIGHT SIDE: With No. 8 (4 mm) needles cast on 179 (189) (199) (209) sts.
Place pattern thus: **1st row (wrong side):** K2, [p7, k3] to last 7 sts, p7. **2nd row:** [Skpo, k3, k2tog, p3] to last 9 sts, skpo, k3, k2tog, p2. These 2 rows place pattern. Continue to match left side of border, noting position of p2 at one edge of work is reversed.

BUTTONHOLE BAND

With No. 8 (4 mm) needles cast on 7 sts. Single rib 4 (6) (4) (6) rows as on back.

Buttonhole row: Rib 3, yf, k2tog, rib 2. Rib 13 (13) (15) (15) rows. Work last 14 (14) (16) (16) rows 3 times more, then work buttonhole row again. Rib 3 (5) (3) (5) rows. Cast off ribwise.

BUTTON BAND

Work as buttonhole band, omitting buttonholes.

TO MAKE UP

Press as given on ball band. Join shoulder seams. Sew front bands to straight edges of fronts.
Beginning and ending at centre of front bands, sew shaped edge of collar to neck, easing in fullness at back. Join the p2 ends of collar edging to form centre back neck seam and sew cast-off edge to collar. Sew cast-off edge of sleeves to row-ends between markers on back and fronts. Join side and sleeve seams. Add buttons.

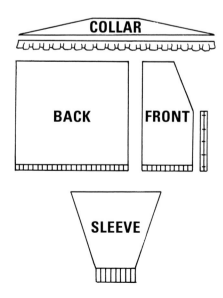

117

FULL STEAM AHEAD

THOMAS THE TANK ENGINE AND FRIENDS ARE ON TRACK FOR THIS CHEERY CARDIGAN

MEASUREMENTS To fit sizes 56 (61) (66) cm/22 (24) (26) in.

Actual measurement 59 (64) (69) cm/23¼ (25¼) (27¼) in. **Side seam** 23.5 (25) (27) cm/9¼ (10) (10¾) in.

Length 37.5 (40.5) (43.5) cm/14¾ (16) (17¼) in. **Sleeve seam** 23.5 (26.5) (29.5) cm/9¼ (10½) (11½) in.

MATERIALS

Allow the following quantities in 50 g balls of Robin New World D.K: 2 green (3355) and 1 blue (3364) for 56 cm/22 in and 61 cm/24 in sizes; 2 green and 2 blue for 66 cm/26 in size. For any one size: 1 ball each of the same yarn in natural (3392), black (3309), red (3328), yellow (3347), white (3301), grey (3303) and brown (3339); a pair each of No. 9 (3¾ mm) and No. 10 (3¼ mm)

knitting needles; 6 buttons. Key: green = g, blue = bl, white = w, natural = n.
For stockists, write to Robert Glew Group, Idle, Bradford, West Yorkshire BD10 9TE.

TENSION

23 stitches and 30 rows, to 10 x 10 cm/4 x 4 in, over stocking stitch, using No. 9 (3¾ mm) needles.

NOTE

Instructions are given for 56 cm (22 inch) size. Where they vary, work figures in round brackets for larger sizes.

The front of this stocking stitch cardigan features James and the Fat Controller, and Thomas is on the back; the characters are worked from easy-to-follow charts. The cardigan has set-in sleeves, and buttons to a round neck. The yarn is machine-washable, acrylic-wool D.K.

BACK

With No. 10 (3¼ mm) needles and g cast on 67 (73) (79) sts and, beginning odd-numbered rows with k1 and even-numbered rows with p1, single rib 12 (16) (18) rows.
Change to No. 9 (3¾ mm) needles and beginning with a k row, ss nil (2) (6) rows.
Continuing in ss, joining and breaking colours as required and using a separate ball of yarn for each colour section, work 58 rows of chart C (Thomas), reading odd-numbered rows from right to left and even-numbered rows from left to right. When changing colours, wind yarn round one just used to avoid leaving a gap.
SHAPE ARMHOLES: Cast off 3 (4) (5) sts at beginning of next 2 rows, following rows 59 and 60 of chart C. Using bl only, dec 1 st each end of next 3 rows, then the following alternate row – 53 (57) (61) sts.
Ss 31 (35) (39) rows.
FOR SHOULDERS: Cast off 8 (8) (9) sts at beginning of next 2 rows and 8 (9) (9) sts on following 2 rows. Leave remaining 21 (23) (25) sts on a spare needle.

LEFT FRONT

With No. 10 (3¼ mm) needles and g cast on 31 (35) (37) sts and work 12 (16) (18) rows in rib as on back, increasing 1 (nil) (1) st at end of last row – 32 (35) (38) sts. **.
Change to No. 9 (3¾ mm) needles and ss 23

(25) (29) rows n, then 2 rows with w. Beginning with a p row, work 33 rows of chart B (James).
TO SHAPE ARMHOLE: Continue working from chart B, cast off 3 (4) (5) sts at beginning of next row. Work 1 row, then dec 1 st at armhole edge on next 3 rows, then the following alternate row – 25 (27) (29) sts.
*** Ss 16 (20) (24) rows – ss 17 (21) (25) rows here for right front.
SHAPE NECK: Cast off 3 (4) (5) sts at beginning of next row, then dec 1 st at neck edge on next 5 rows, then the following alternate row – 16 (17) (18) sts. Ss 7 rows.
FOR SHOULDER: Cast off 8 (8) (9) sts at beginning of next row. Work 1 row. Cast off 8 (9) (9) sts.

RIGHT FRONT

Work as left front to **.
Change to No. 9 (3¾ mm) needles and ss nil (2) (6) rows with n.
Work 59 rows from chart A (Fat Controller).
SHAPE ARMHOLE: Cast off 3 (4) (5) sts at beginning of next row, following 60th row of chart A.
With bl, dec 1 st at armhole edge on next 3 rows and then the following alternate row – 25 (27) (29) sts. Work as left front from *** to end, noting variation.

SLEEVES

With No. 10 (3¼ mm) needles and g cast on 33 (35) (37) sts and work 12 (16) (18) rows in rib as on back.
Change to No. 9 (3¾ mm) needles and ss 4 rows. Inc 1 st at each end of next row and 3 (5) (7) following 4th rows, then the 5 following 6th rows – 51 (57) (63) sts. Ss 9 (7) (7) rows.
Work skyline thus: **1st row:** K4 (7) (10) bl, 41 g, 6 (9) (12) bl. **2nd row:** P9 (12) (15) bl, 8

g, 5 bl, 24 g, 5 (8) (11) bl.
SHAPE SLEEVE TOP: 1st row: With bl, cast off 3
(4) (5), k next 3 (5) (7) bl, 5 g, 9 bl, 7 g, 7
bl, 5 g, 11 (14) (17) bl. **2nd row**: With bl,
cast off 3 (4) (5), p next 21 (23) (25) bl, 4
g, 19 (21) (23) bl.
With bl, dec 1 st at each end of next row
and 7 (9) (11) following alternate rows – 29
sts.
Work 1 row, cast off 3 sts at beginning of
next 4 rows. Cast off 17 sts.

NECKBAND

Join shoulder seams. With right side facing,
rejoin bl and using No. 10 (3¼ mm) needles,
pick up and k21 (22) (23) sts up right front
neck, k across 21 (23) (25) sts at back neck,
pick up and k21 (22) (23) sts down left front
neck – 63 (67) (71) sts. Work 6 rows in rib
as on back. Cast off in rib.

BUTTON BORDER

With No. 10 (3¼ mm) needles and g cast on
9 sts and with g, work 12 (16) (18) rows in
rib as on back, rib 23 (25) (29) rows with n,
2 rows with w, 33 rows with g and 30 (34)
(38) rows with bl. Cast off in rib.

BUTTONHOLE BORDER

With No. 10 (3¼ mm) needles and g cast on
9 sts and work in rib and colour sequence as
given for button border, rib 4 rows.
1st buttonhole row: Rib 3, cast off 3, rib to end.
2nd buttonhole row: Rib to end, casting on 3 sts
over those cast off on previous row. Rib 16
(18) (20) rows. Repeat last 18 (20) (22)
rows, 4 times more, then 2 buttonhole rows
again. Rib 4 rows. Cast off in rib.

TO MAKE UP

Press. Set in sleeves, then join sleeve and side
seams. Sew on borders, placing buttonholes
on appropriate front. Using straight sts,
embroider Thomas' and James' faces with w
and black yarn. Outline number and Thomas
engine front between black and bl sections
with red, mark centre of Thomas' wheels
with 2 black sts. Outline James' engine face
with black. Add buttons.

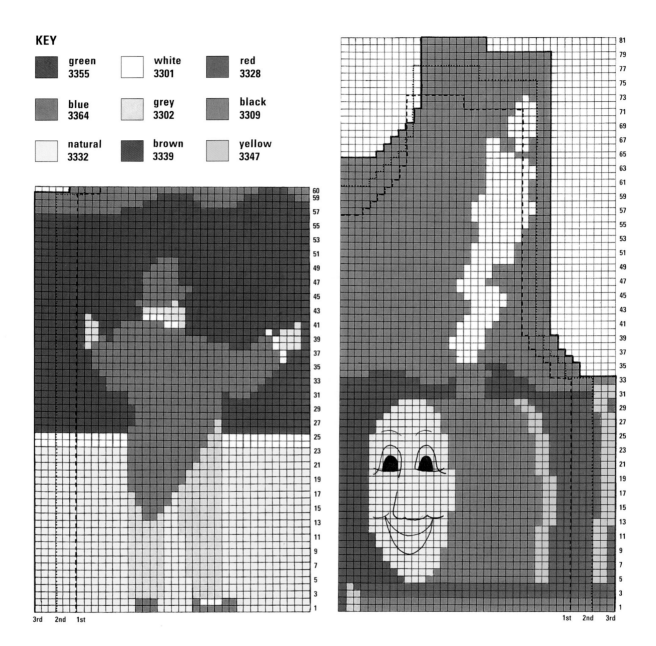

KEY

green 3355	white 3301	red 3328
blue 3364	grey 3302	black 3309
natural 3332	brown 3339	yellow 3347

KNITTING KNOW-HOW

TENSION

Tension is the most important word in both knitting and crochet. The term is both used to describe the number of stitches and rows produced to a certain measurement, using a given size of needles, a specified yarn and a particular stitch pattern.

A garment can be made and completed beautifully, but if the tension is not correct, the results are disastrous, the garment being either far too large or much too small.

Unfortunately, the only advice to be given on such occasions is to unravel and begin again once the correct tension has been established

Before beginning any pattern, knit up a sample square using the correct yarn and needles, casting on enough stitches to measure at least 10 x 10 cm (4 x 4in) according to the "tension" paragraph given at the start of each pattern.

If the sample square measures less than it should, the knitting is too tight and larger needles should be used to try again. If the sample square measures more than it should, the knitting is too loose and you should try again using smaller needles.

Obtaining the correct tension on a tension square does not guarantee a stable tension all through the garment. Check it at regular intervals during the making of your garment to ensure the correct tension is being maintained.

PICKING UP STITCHES

This is mainly required for neckbands and front borders. Work with the right side of the fabric facing, unless otherwise stated.

Begin by dividing the edge of the fabric into equal sections with pins as markers and pick up the same amount of stitches from each section to obtain an evenly spaced edging.

When picking up stitches from a straight edge, you can insert the needle either between or into each stitch as long as you are consistent and keep to the chosen system all along the row. A curved edge is worked in a similar way, but the needle should be inserted into the middle of each stitch where possible.

Pick-up-row: * Insert the needle into the chosen place from front to back, take yarn round point of needle at back of work and draw a loop through to the right side; repeat from * to end.

SELECTING YOUR YARN

It is important to obtain the correct yarn quoted in the pattern. Unfortunately, in many instances time, effort and money can be wasted if this point is disregarded.

Some basic yarns such as 4-ply, double knitting and aran can on occasions be substituted, but it is advisable first to buy one ball of the chosen yarn to test the tension. If the tension quoted is obtained and the resulting fabric is acceptable, then the garment should knit to similar measurements to those given in the "measurements" chart. As even basic yarns differ in content, such as 100% wool as opposed to 100% acrylic, the yardage may not be the same in the substitute yarn, so more or less yarn may be required.

Speciality yarns such as Mohair, fluffy and knobbly textures are not ideal yarns to substitute as no two yarns are exactly the same in weight and finish, and once knitted up, can prove very difficult to unravel and the surface of the yarn can be damaged in the process.

It is impossible for each yarn shop to stock all of the many ranges that are produced today, and if a substitute yarn is obtained, the results cannot be guaranteed. For this reason the address of each spinner concerned has been included in the "materials" paragraph of all patterns. They will be happy either to give details of the local stockist where the specified yarn can be obtained or they may offer a postal service.

JOINING NEW YARN

Where possible it is advisable to join in a new ball of yarn at the beginning of a row. Knot the new yarn around the one just used and push the knot up close to the needle. The ends can then be woven in to the seams at the make up stage.

If the yarn has to be joined in the middle of a row, the "splicing" method is suitable on most occasions. Unravel the two ends to be joined for approximately 10 cm (4 in) and cut away half of the strands from each end. Overlay the remaining strands in opposite directions and twist them together to obtain a similar thickness to the original yarn. Knit the next few stitches very carefully until the "join" has been passed.

THE MAKING UP

There are several ways to join the seams together and most people have their own favourite way. Detailed instructions of three different methods have been included, which should be worked with a blunt-ended wool needle using either the original yarn or a finer thread of the same colour.

FLAT SEAM: This is useful for fine lacy work where a seam could show through and is worked with the right side of the fabric facing.

Lay the two pieces of fabric side by side, * insert needle into the next edge loop of the first side and draw thread through, then insert needle into the adjacent edge loop of the second side and draw thread through; repeat from * to end, working towards the left.

INVISIBLE SEAM: This is useful where two straight edges are to be joined, such as side seams in a sweater, and is worked with the right side of the fabric facing.

Lay the two pieces of fabric side by side. Work consistently either in the centre of each stitch or between stitches so that when the edges are drawn together, the join disappears.

* Insert the needle under a stitch on first side and draw thread through, then insert needle under adjacent stitch on second side and draw thread through; draw up thread so that the stitches on the main fabric side are touching and the edge stitches sink to the back; repeat from * to end working towards the left.

BACK STITCH SEAM: This is useful where there are shaped edges, such as setting in sleeves or sleeve seams, and is worked on the wrong side of the fabric.

Place the two edges of fabric with right sides together, and work seam approximately 5 mm (¼ in) in from the edges.

Insert needle through the 2 thicknesses of fabric and bring it through two stitches to the left; draw thread through; * take needle back across front of the work 2 stitches to the right and insert at the end of the previous stitch worked; bring needle through four stitches to the left; repeat from * to end.

PRESSING AND AFTERCARE

If the yarn used requires pressing, block out each piece of fabric to shape and size with wrong side uppermost, using plenty of pins at regular intervals.

Most manufacturers give advice on the ball band for pressing and washing, which should be followed most carefully for your garment to retain its freshness. Once a yarn has been pressed wrongly and the fabric has gone "flat", no amount of washing can bring back the soft springy feeling that the garment began with.

This also applies to the washing. Many of the curtain yarns are machine washable and are easily maintained, but there are equally as many that should be hand washed only.

When giving a hand knitted garment as a gift, it is useful to include a ball band so that the after-care instructions are passed on to the new owner.

KNITTING ABBREVIATIONS

Please read abbreviations before working.

Standard abbreviations

dec, decrease (by taking 2 sts tog); dmst, double moss st; double rib is k2 and p2 alternately; gst, garter st (k plain on every row); inc, increase (by working twice into same st); k, knit; k or p1b, k or p1 through back of stitch; k2togb, k2tog through back of sts; mst, moss st; nil, meaning nothing is worked here for this size; p, purl; psso, pass sl st over; rss, reverse stocking st (p on right side and k on wrong side); single rib is k1 and p1 alternately; skpo, (sl1, k1, pass sl st over); sl, slip; ss, stocking st (k on right side and p on wrong side); st, stitch; tog, together; twisted single rib is k1b and p1 alternately; up1, pick up loop lying between needles and k or p into back of it.

Country Classic p6

cr2rt, cross 2 right (sl next st on to cable needle and leave at back, k1, then k st from cable needle); cr2lt, cross 2 left (as cr2rt, but leave cable needle at front); mb, make bobble (k1, p1, k1, p1 all into next st, then pass 2nd, 3rd and 4th sts over 1st st); c4b, cable 4 back (sl next 2 sts on to cable needle and leave at back, k2, then k2 from cable needle); c4f, cable 4 front (as c4b, but leave cable needle at front).

Instant Impact p10

yf, yarn to front of work; yon, yarn over needle to make a st.

Pale Perfection p14

c4b, cable 4 back (sl 2 sts on cable needle and leave at back, k2, then k2 from cable needle); c4f, cable 4 front (as c4b, but leave cable needle at front); cr4rt, cross 4 right (sl 2 sts on cable needle and leave at back k2, then p2 from cable needle); cr4lt, cross 4 left (sl 2 sts on cable needle and leave at front, p2, then k2 from cable needle); tw2, twist 2 (sl 1 st on cable needle and leave at back, k1, then k1 from cable needle).

Golden Glow p18

k1b, k1 below (k into next st, 1 row below st on needle).

Stylish Waistcoat p22

c6b, cable 6 back (sl next 3 sts on cable needle and leave at back, k3, then k3 from cable needle); c6f, cable 6 front (as C6b, but leave cable needle at front).

Mellow Moods p26

up 1, pick up loop lying between needles and work into back of it; cr4lt, cross 4 left (sl next 3 sts on to cable needle and leave at front, k1, then k1b, p1, k1b from cable needle); cr4rt, cross 4 right (sl next st on to cable needle and leave at back,
k1b, p1, k1b, then k st from cable needle); tw2rt, twist 2 right (k2 tog, but do not sl sts off left-hand needle, k into front of 1st st, then sl both sts off needle tog); tw2lt, twist 2 left (k into back of 2nd st on left-hand needle, then k 1st and 2nd sts tog through back, sl both sts off left-hand needle); yf, yarn forward to make a st; mb, make bobble (k1, yf, k1, yf, k1 all into same st, turn, p5, turn, k3, k2 tog, then pass the 3rd, 2nd, and 1st k sts over k2 tog).

Tops for Texture p30

k2togb, k2tog through back of sts; k1 or 2b, k1 or 2 through back of sts; p1 or 2b, p1 or 2 through back of sts; cr5k, cross 5 knit (sl 3 sts on cable needle and leave at front, k2, sl end st from cable needle back on left-hand needle, k this st, then k2 sts from cable needle); cr5p, cross 5 purl (sl 3 sts on cable needle and leave at front, k2b, sl end st from cable needle back on left-hand needle, p this st, then k2b from cable needle); tw2, twist 2 (sl 1 st on cable needle and leave at front, k1b, then k1b from cable needle); tw2b, twist 2 back (sl 1 st on cable needle and leave at back, k1b, then p1 from cable needle); tw2f, twist 2 front (sl 1 st on cable needle and leave at front, p1, then k1b from cable needle); mb, make bobble (k1, p1, k1, p1 all in next st, [turn p4, turn, k4] twice, sl last 3 sts over 1st st); 3 from 1, (k1, p1, k1 all in same st); tw3b, twist 3 back (sl 1 st on cable needle and leave at back, k2b, then p1 from cable needle); tw3f, twist 3 front (sl 2 sts on cable needle and leave at front, p1, then k2b from cable needle).

Laced with Cream p34

 k or p1b, k or p1 through back of st; cr2rt, cross 2 right (sl 1 st on cable needle and leave at back k1, then p1 from cable needle); cr2lt, cross 2 left (sl 1 st on cable needle and leave at front, p1, then k1 from cable needle); tw2rt, twist 2 right (sl 1 st on cable needle and leave at back, k1, then k1 from cable needle); tw2lt, twist 2 left (sl 1 st on cable needle and leave at front, k1, then k1 from cable needle); mb, make bobble (k1, p1, k1, p1, k1, p1, k1 all into next st, then sl last 6 sts all over 1st st); yf, yarn forward; yon, yarn over needle; yrn, yarn round needle.

Nice and Easy p38

up1k, pick up the loop lying between needles and k into back of it; up1p, pick up the loop lying between the needles and p into back of it.

Splash of Scarlet p42

yf, yarn forward to make a st.

Silky Touch p46

c5rt, cross 5 right (sl next 2 sts onto cable needle and leave at back, k3, then p2 from cable needle); c5lt, cross 5 left (sl 3 sts onto cable needle and leave at front, p2, then k3 from cable needle); c6rt, cable 6 right (sl 3 sts onto cable needle and leave at back, k3 then k3 from cable needle); c6lt, cable 6 left (sl 3 sts onto cable needle and leave at front, k3, then k3 from cable needle);

c8rt, cross 8 right (sl 5 sts onto cable needle and leave at back, k3, then k3, p2 from cable needle; c8lt, cross 8 left (sl 3 sts onto cable needle and leave at front, p2, k3, then k3 from cable needle).

Cream Cables p50

c4f, cable 4 front (slip next 2 sts on to cable needle and leave at front, k2, then k2 from cable needle).

Out of the Blue p 54

yf, yarn foward; yrn, yarn round needle; tw3l, twist 3 left (sl 2 sts on cable needle and leave at front, p1, then k2 from cable needle); tw3r, twist 3 right (sl 1 st on cable needle and leave at back, k2, then p1 from cable needle).

Classic Cardigan p62

c6b, cable 6 back (sl 3 sts on to cable and leave at back, k3, then k3 from cable needle); c6f, cable 6 front (as c6b, but leave cable needle at front).

Perfect Mix p66

yf, yarn forward to make a st; c4b, cable 4 back (sl 2 sts on to cable needle and leave at back, k2, then k2 from cable needle); cr3lt, cross 3 left (sl 2 sts on to cable needle and leave at front, k1, then k2 from cable needle); cr3rt, cross 3 right (sl 1 st on to cable needle and leave at back, k2, then k st from cable needle); tw3rt, twist 3 right (sl 1 st on to cable needle and leave at back, k2, then p st from cable needle); tw3lt, twist 3 left (sl 2 sts on to cable needle and leave at front, p1, then k2 from cable needle); single rib is k1 and p1, alternately.

Scottish Style p74

inc, increase (by working twice into next st).

Boy Blue p86

cr4rt, cross 4 right (sl next st on to cable needle and leave at back, k1b, p1, k1b, then p1 from cable needle); cr4lt, cross 4 left (sl next 3 sts on to cable needle and leave at front, p1, then k1b, p1, k1b from cable needle); cr7, cross 7 (sl next 3 sts on to cable needle and leave at front, k1b, p1, k1b, p1, then k1b, p1, k1b from cable needle).

Baby Grand p90

yf, yarn foward to make a st; yrn, yarn round need to make a st.

Bobble Top p94

mb, make bobble (k into front, back, front, back of next st, turn, p4, turn, k4, turn, p2tog, p2tog, turn, sl1, k1, pass sl st over.

Buttons and Bows p106

 c4, cable 4 (sl 2 sts on to cable needle and leave at front, k2 then k2 from cable needle).

Beautiful Brownie p 114

c3bp, cable 3 back p (sl 1 st on cable needle, leave at back, k2, then p st from cable needle); c3fp, cable 3 front p (sl 2 sts on cable needle, leave at front, p1, then k2 from cable needle); c3b, cable 3 back (sl 1 st on cable needle, leave at back, k2, then k1 from cable needle); c3f, cable 3 front (sl 2 sts on cable needle, leave at front, k1, then k2 from cable needle); c4f, cable 4 front (sl 2 sts on cable needle, leave at front, p2, then k2 from cable needle); c4b, cable 4 back (sl 2 sts on cable needle, leave at back, k2, then p2 from cable needle); yf, yarn forward to make a st.

INDEX

ACKNOWLEDGEMENTS

Picture Credits

Key: p PHOTOGRAPHER; s STYLIST; h HAIR AND MAKE-UP

7 p Paul Viant s Angela Kennedy h Barbara Jones; 10 p Dave Anthony s Angela Kennedy h Barbara Jones; 15 p Dave Anthony s Angela Kennedy h Barbara Jones; 18 p Chris Edwick s Angela Kennedy h Dotty Monaghan; 23 p Dave Anthony s Angela Kennedy h Kay Fielding; 26 p Colin Thomas s Clare Grundy h Kaz Simler; 31 p Dave Anthony s Angela Kennedy h Barbara Jones; 34 h Dotty Monaghan; 42 p Chris Edwick s Angela Kennedy h Barbara Jones; 50 p Dave Anthony s Julie Player h Dotty Monaghan; 63 p Dave Anthony s Angela Kennedy h Kay Fielding; 71 p Mike Prior h Randy Chartrand; 74 p Chris Edwick s Angela Kennedy; 79 p Paul Viant s Angela Kennedy h Dotty Monaghan; 87 p Sarah Hutchings s Angela Kennedy; 93 p Marie-Louise Avery s Angela Kennedy; 95 p Paul Viant s Angela Kennedy h Dotty Monaghan; 112 p Colin Thomas s Julie Player h Francis Leinster; 114 p Dave Anthony s Angela Kennedy; 119 p Tex Ritter s Linda Mindel-Carvell.
The publishers apologise for any unintentional omissions to the above picture credits and would be pleased to insert the appropriate acknowledgements in any subsequent editions.

Wilf took a tent round to Chip's house. He and Chip were going to sleep in it.

"I've never slept in a tent before," said Chip. "I wonder what it will be like?"

"It will be fun," said Wilf. "But we'll need a survival kit."

Wilf had lots of things in a rucksack.

"These can go in our survival kit," he said. "We'll need them to survive outside. I've got a torch, a ball of string, a plastic sheet, some chocolate and a first aid box. What else will we need to survive?"

"I've got a mirror, a pencil and notebook, and a bag of crisps," said Chip.

Biff came out with a big umbrella. "You might need this. It's going to rain," she said.

"You can't have an umbrella in a survival kit," said Wilf. "Don't be silly, Biff."

That evening, it began to rain. It rained so
hard that Chip and Wilf couldn't sleep outside in
the tent.

In the end, Mum said they could camp on
Chip's bedroom floor.

"You won't need a survival kit here," said Biff.

Suddenly, the magic key began to glow.
The children were pulled into a new adventure.

"If this is going to be a survival adventure,"
said Biff, "I'm taking the umbrella."

"You won't need an umbrella on a survival
adventure," shouted Chip. "Don't be silly."

Amy was tired and fed up. The wagons were
stuck. They had been stuck for two days.

Amy's family was on a long journey. They were
going to a new land. They were taking everything
in the wagon. They had come a long way and
they had a long way to go.

"Stay close to the wagon train," said Amy's
father. "Don't wander off. It's easy to get lost in
the woods."

Amy didn't listen to her father.

"I'll go and pick some wild berries," she thought.
"If I don't go far, I won't get lost."

Amy found lots of blueberries in the wood, but she didn't stay close to the wagon train. She just went on and on.

"I must get back," she thought at last. But she couldn't find her way. All the trees looked the same. "Oh no! I'm lost!" she thought.

Amy was frightened. She didn't know which
way to go. Suddenly, something closed on her
foot. It was a trap, and she couldn't get it off.

"Help! Help!" shouted Amy. "Help me,
somebody."

But Amy was a long way from the wagon
train and nobody could hear her.

Little Fox was tired and fed up. He had been in the woods all day looking for honey. But he hadn't found any.

Every time he found a tree with a bees' nest, the honey was gone.

Now he was lost.

Little Fox knew why there was no honey.
There was a brown bear in the woods. The bear
had taken all the honey.

Little Fox was frightened. He was a long way
from the village, and the bear was not far away.

"I must be careful," thought Little Fox.

Little Fox heard Amy shouting.

"Someone is in trouble," he thought. He ran through the trees as fast as he could. He found Amy caught in the trap.

Little Fox tried to open the trap, but he wasn't strong enough.

The bear was a long way away, but he heard
Amy shouting too. He stood on his hind legs and
sniffed the air.

The bear could smell Amy and Little Fox.
He was a bad-tempered bear. He didn't like people
in his part of the wood.

The magic key took Biff, Chip and Wilf to
the woods where Little Fox was helping Amy.

Little Fox and Amy were amazed. They had
never seen children like these, before.

Biff, Chip and Wilf were amazed too.

"It looks like they're in trouble," said Chip.

The children could see that Amy was caught
in the trap. They ran to help Little Fox. Together
they pulled open the jaws of the trap.

"Ugh!" said Chip. "What a horrid thing."

"The trappers use them to catch animals,"
said Little Fox. "Traps like this are cruel."

The trap had hurt Amy's leg. Wilf put a
bandage on it.

Biff and Little Fox smashed the trap with a
rock.

"It's a good idea to smash the trap," said Little
Fox, "but we shouldn't make all this noise. The
bear will hear us."

Suddenly, the children heard a roar. The bear
came out of the trees and ran towards them. All
the children were frightened.

"Oh help!" shouted Wilf. "This bear doesn't
look very friendly. Run!"

"I can't," said Amy.

Biff had an idea. She opened the umbrella and
shut it. Then she opened it and spun it round and
round.

The bear stopped. He was afraid of the umbrella.
He had never seen anything like it. Then he gave
a roar and ran away.

"That was brilliant," said Chip. "But how did you know that bears are afraid of umbrellas?"

"I didn't," said Biff.

Suddenly, it began to rain. "Now who says you can't have an umbrella in a survival kit?" she asked. "Don't get wet everyone. Come under the umbrella."

After it stopped raining, the children went on. At last, they came to a river. Little Fox told everyone to keep quiet. Then he lay down on the bank and put his arm in the water. Suddenly, he caught a fish.

"That's amazing," said Chip. "I couldn't do that."

"How do we cook it?" asked Amy. "We don't
have a fire."

But Little Fox made a fire. He made it with a
bow and a stick.

"That's amazing, too," said Chip. "He's lit a
fire without any matches."

It was getting dark and it was beginning to
rain again. Chip and Wilf put up the tent. Biff and
Amy put up the plastic sheet to make a shelter.

Little Fox cooked the fish and the children sat
round the fire. They ate the fish, and the berries
that Amy had picked. Then they ate the
chocolate.

Amy told everyone about her mother and father. She told them how the wagon train had got stuck in the mud.

Amy began to cry.

"Maybe I'll never see my mother and father again," she said.

"Don't worry," said Wilf. "We'll find them."

Suddenly, Biff grabbed the umbrella and jumped to her feet. She ran outside and began to shout.

"Help!" she called. "We've been surrounded."

Everyone jumped up. Biff spun the umbrella round and round.

"Go away! Go away!" she shouted.

Little Fox laughed and laughed. Everyone laughed.

"This is my father," said Little Fox. "He thought I was lost. He was looking for me."

"Sorry!" said Biff.

"You were very brave," said Little Fox's father.

"Yes, she frightened the bear," said Little Fox.

The children told Little Fox's father about
their adventures in the wood. They told him
about the trap. He laughed when they told him
how the bear was afraid of Biff's umbrella.

"It's easy to get lost in the woods," said Little
Fox's father.

Amy told Little Fox's father about the wagon
train.

"My mother and father will be worried about
me," she said. "They will think I have been killed
by a bear."

"Don't worry," said Little Fox's father. "We will
soon find the wagon train."

In the morning, Little Fox's father found the
wagon train. Amy's mother and father were glad
that Amy was safe.

"We looked and looked for you in the woods,"
said her father. "When we couldn't find you we
thought you had been killed by a bear."

"I almost was," said Amy.

The wagons were still stuck. "We've been stuck like this for three days," said Amy's father.

Little Fox looked at his father. "Can't we help?" he said. "Can't we all help pull them out?"

Little Fox's father laughed. He spoke to his men. Soon they pulled the wagons out of the mud.

At last, the wagon train was able to go on. The children watched them for a long time.

"I wouldn't like to be on that wagon train," said Biff. "It will be a hard journey. There are no shops to buy food. And there isn't a doctor if they are ill."

The magic key began to glow. It was time for
the adventure to end. Biff gave Little Fox the umbrella.

"You can use it to frighten away the bears,"
she laughed.

Biff looked at Wilf and Chip.

"Umbrellas are useful in a survival kit after all,"
she said.

The children liked the survival adventure.
The next day, they put the tent up. Biff wanted
to make Wilf and Chip laugh.

"Look what's outside!" she said. "And I haven't
got my umbrella, now."

"Oh no," laughed Wilf. "What shall we do?
We can't survive without Biff's umbrella."